TO MY DAUGHTERS, WITH LOVE

By Pearl S. Buck

FOR SPACIOUS SKIES
  [with Theodore F. Harris]
THE GIFTS THEY BRING
  [with Gweneth T. Zarfoss]
THE JOY OF CHILDREN
FRIEND TO FRIEND
  [with Carlos P. Romulo]
MY SEVERAL WORLDS
THE CHILD WHO NEVER GREW

AMERICAN ARGUMENT
TALK ABOUT RUSSIA
WHAT AMERICA MEANS TO ME
OF MEN AND WOMEN
HOW IT HAPPENS
TELL THE PEOPLE
AMERICAN UNITY AND ASIA
FIGHTING ANGEL
THE EXILE

THE CHINESE NOVEL [NOBEL PRIZE LECTURE]

THE TIME IS NOON
DEATH IN THE CASTLE
THE LIVING REED
FOURTEEN STORIES
COMMAND THE MORNING
LETTER FROM PEKING
COME MY BELOVED
IMPERIAL WOMAN
THE HIDDEN FLOWER
GOD'S MEN
PAVILION OF WOMEN

KINFOLK
FAR AND NEAR
PEONY
VOICES IN THE HOUSE
BRIGHT PROCESSION

PORTRAIT OF A MARRIAGE
THE PROMISE
DRAGON SEED
TODAY AND FOREVER
OTHER GODS
THE PATRIOT
THIS PROUD HEART
A HOUSE DIVIDED
THE MOTHER
THE FIRST WIFE AND OTHER
  STORIES
SONS
THE GOOD EARTH
EAST WIND: WEST WIND
THE TOWNSMAN
THE LONG LOVE
THE ANGRY WIFE

ALL MEN ARE BROTHERS [SHUI HU CHÜAN] translated from the
  Chinese

MATTHEW, MARK, LUKE
  AND JOHN
THE BIG FIGHT
WELCOME CHILD
THE CHRISTMAS GHOST
CHRISTMAS MINIATURE
MY SEVERAL WORLDS
  [Abridged for Younger
  Readers]
THE BEECH TREE

JOHNNY JACK AND HIS
  BEGINNINGS
ONE BRIGHT DAY
THE BIG WAVE
YU LAN: FLYING BOY OF CHINA
THE DRAGON FISH
THE WATER-BUFFALO CHILDREN
THE CHINESE CHILDREN NEXT
  DOOR
STORIES FOR LITTLE CHILDREN

TO
MY DAUGHTERS,
WITH LOVE

Pearl S. Buck

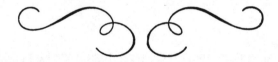

THE JOHN DAY COMPANY
NEW YORK

The author gratefully acknowledges the courtesy of The World Publishing Company in permitting inclusion of a passage from *Man's Most Dangerous Myth*, by Ashley Montagu, and of Random House, Inc., for a portion of "Our Sexual Revolution" which appeared in *Children for Adoption*, by Pearl S. Buck (Copyright © 1964 by Pearl S. Buck).

Library of Congress Catalogue
Number: 67–24634
MANUFACTURED IN THE UNITED STATES OF AMERICA

To My Seven Daughters

Contents

9

Foreword

Blessed am I, for I have seven daughters. The eldest is eighteen years older than the youngest, the youngest is eighteen years younger than the eldest, and together they span some four decades. Each daughter is different from every other, and each one has been a new experience for me, a new education, a new enrichment of life. The eldest, my only birth child, has phenylketonuria. This defect has led me into the world of biochemists, of parents and teachers of retarded children, and the heartbreaking bravery of the mentally retarded themselves. The next daughter, tall and handsome, is a successful professional in the field of occupational therapy. She has broadened my life to include the mentally ill and the aged. The next one, the dark-haired one with violet eyes, has led me into the delightful world of motherhood, she with her five children, and beyond that the teaching of several others in nursery school and kindergarten. The four younger ones are my world children, the eldest of them, now twenty, uniting Germany and America in her ancestry, and the other three, aged sixteen, eighteen and nineteen, bringing

Asia and America together in a union indissoluble. They are all beautiful to see, delightful to live with in our house. Even a problem can be exciting.

In the years together we have talked our way through life and around the world, for we are an articulate group and we argue and discuss and discover solutions to the various problems of our personal lives, as well as the universal problems we see anywhere in the world. From such shared talk I learn and, being a writer above all else, I have distilled articles and essays, and stories and speeches, in a fashion, making my own conclusions in this book which in honesty I must dedicate to my daughters since they are the ones who persuaded me, stimulated me and in some instances goaded me to the final writing. Some of these speeches were commencement addresses, given at their various graduation ceremonies.

I have sons, also, and they have their value and are also indispensable. This book, however, is properly dedicated to daughters; and seven I have not found too many since they have opened for me seven gates to life, each unique. To each I give my thanks.

Dear Daughters, this is your book. Share it as you will with those who are to be its readers.

Pearl S. Buck

ON YOUTH

I

To the Young

IF I had some magic way to reach the ear of every young man and woman today, in every country, what would I say?

In a degree, all young people in every country are in the same predicament. They have been taught and trained for a world which they find does not exist. They have grown up to discover themselves without the tools of thought and action necessary for their lives. The era has suddenly and abruptly changed within a few years. The young people of Germany, after World War II, must have found this especially true. Much that they had been taught in and out of school could not be used. They were faced with a strange and unhappy world, one in which they had at once less freedom and more freedom. They had those who are foreign sitting in power, and yet those same foreigners expected from them a kind of independence which they were not able to exert. The destruction of ideals, whether those ideals were right or wrong, must also have been a shock to the mind and the heart. Life without idealism is empty indeed. We must have hope as we must have bread; to eat bread without hope is still slowly to starve to death.

Yet the predicament which faced the youth of Germany is in some measure that which faces all youth everywhere. In China youth was full of despair, or they would not have yielded to Communism. In Japan, the young were as the young in Germany. They, too, were educated for a world now gone. In India, the young are full of hope, for they see an independence, however limited, for their people. Yet they are weighed down by centuries of misrule and poverty and illiteracy, and it can hardly be hoped that within their generation they will see anything but struggle. Even in the United States, this country, which is considered so fortunate and which is fortunate, the young have been much bewildered. That hope of one world, that dream of real brotherhood, that belief in human equality which is the natural feeling of most young Americans, these ideals have been rudely shaken in the years since the war. Young Americans have watched, even in their own country, the development of a divided world, the rise of militarism instead of brotherhood, the insistence upon selfish interests rather than upon human welfare. They, too, feel that their education and training were not for such a world as this.

It is natural that the young, therefore, should everywhere feel confused and frightened and even angry. Certainly they feel they have not been taught rightly and that things are not right in the world. It is well that they feel so. Did all young people feel complacent and satisfied now, then indeed there would be no hope for humanity.

The hope for mankind lies in the rebellion of the young against the individual selfishness, the nationalism, the inequalities of the present. Upon the profound discontent of the young in every country do I set my faith. I beg you, the young, to be discontented. I pray that you may rebel against what is wrong, not with feeble negative complaining but with strong positive assertion of what is right for all humanity.

The greatest evil that has been done to the young has been in their education. It is difficult indeed to struggle against what one has been taught. The child's mind is a helpless one, pliable, absorbing. It makes what it learns a part of its very nature, so that those who have been taught an overweening nationalism will find it difficult to think in terms of all the peoples of the world. Yet what is good for one people is good for all, and none will be safe anywhere until all are safe everywhere. That Jews could be so ruthlessly killed in Germany, that Negroes could be so ruthlessly lynched in the United States, that Hindus and Moslems could be killed in India, that any can be hunted down for what they believe in religion or politics, means that all can suffer such wrongs somewhere, sometimes. None of us is safe until the great basic laws of humanity are established for all the peoples of the world by all the peoples of the world.

Food for all is a necessity. Food should not be a merchandise, to be bought and sold as jewels are bought and sold by those who have the money to buy. Food is a human necessity, like water and air, and it should be as available. Education is a necessity for the human mind, health is a necessity for the human body, and these should be made available for all human creatures everywhere.

Above all, the human creature needs freedom to be himself, freedom to speak what is in his mind, freedom to act as he wills, freedom to come and go, freedom for fair trial and just judgment, freedom to live, and these freedoms only come with good government—a government which exists to serve the people and not to rule them. Such freedom is limited only by the freedom for each individual. One human being may not use his freedom to curtail the happiness and freedom of others. It is the only limitation upon individual independence.

These are not complex and impossible ideals. They are all quite simple and quite within the realm of possibility and on a world scale, if the world is conceived of as one community—which indeed it is—with separate homes for the nation-citizens. What keeps these ideals from being realized is the nationalism which strives to rule instead of to cooperate. Many nations have been guilty of this greedy desire to have more power, more material goods, more freedom than others around them. Within every nation are individuals who are guilty of this same greed for more than their share. These nations, these individuals, must not be allowed to fulfill their ambitions at the expense of others. Never should they be allowed to come to a place of leadership in the world.

The test of all leaders is this: Do they think in terms of themselves and their own or do they think in terms of the world and humanity? Today, to dream of nationalism is obsolete. The whole struggle is between this old, dead nationalism and the new concept of the world community. The new era has begun. No era begins clean and whole. There is always a period of transition when the old ways cling and old individuals live on. But the old era is gone, for all that, and the new era is here.

I think in some ways that the United States, my own country, is and will be the slowest of all countries to realize that the new era is here. We suffered less than most peoples from the war. We have not made a clean break with the old era of empires and nationalisms. We have not absolutely seen the folly of aggressive militarism in a world already sick and starving and homeless because of militarism rampant. It may be that the leadership toward this new era will not come from us. I grieve to think that this may be so. I hope it will—I hope we can learn quickly enough.

To me, human beings are human beings. I do not ask their country, their nation, their race, their creed. We are all the same wherever we are, creatures born into this world for a short space, coming from where we do not know and going to the unknown. How can we live in this little time so that we can get the most happiness and good for ourselves? We can get this happiness and good only as we get it for all, in equal measure. The profound satisfaction of seeing people happy and gay and comfortable, well fed and free, makes one's own happiness real, one's own freedom secure. It is the only happiness—the only security. It is the new era. Either we go on to this new era

or we sink back into the old morass of miserable bar-
barism where man becomes the beast, and hunting man,
the beast.

Yet nowhere have our young people been trained for
this world community. I am asking you, young people, to
dream of a world of which you have not heard; to work
for a world with techniques which you have never been
taught. You must change your minds, you must renew
your hearts, and you must do it alone. There are no
teachers for you. Your old teachers are no use to you, for
they did not know how to train you for this new era, this
world mind. Your new teachers, alas, will not suffice. You
must dream your own dreams, you must think out your
own ways of fulfilling them, and then you must try to
make the dreams real and the work practical.

What I say is—it can be done, and it must be done if
humanity is to be saved. Saved for what? Saved for the joy
that is life! Yes, life can be and should be a joy. We are
part of the life of a vast universe, and because life can be
a happy and good experience, it ought to be happy and
good. The ways are simple, our needs are few; food for
the growth of mind and body, and freedom in which to
grow—that is all. Growth itself contains the germ of
happiness. Therefore we must make good growth possible
for all, and in that very work of making it possible for
others and for all, we make it possible, nay inevitable, for
ourselves.

2

To a Daughter

MY VERY DEAR:

I am pleased, of course, that your senior class in high school has asked me to make your Commencement address. You were thoughtful enough to send me the invitation six months ago, giving me, you said, plenty of time to prepare what I wanted to say. In actuality, I am not sure it has been a kindness to provide me with so much time for thought. It has also provided time for doubt.

What can I talk about? Is there anything that I might say which can be of use to you and your classmates, or even of interest to you? I remember a letter you sent me in your freshman year.

Apropos of nothing, it seemed to me then, you wrote: "I can only learn from my own experience." It was a warning to me that everything I have tried to teach you was to be tested by your own experience before you would believe it. I replied by return mail that each generation must learn from the preceding one, else there can be no human progress. In fact, your whole practical life is built upon what others before you have learned and have taught you and which you now use, almost without thought.

It is only in the area of morals and ethics that it seems you refuse to accept universal knowledge. Here you claim the right to question, to disbelieve, to denounce, to reject. You have this right, of course. Improvement is always possible in all areas, and to question is the primary step. If there is a better way of doing anything, certainly one must find that way. Yet I venture to suggest that improvement can only be made when it is based upon immutable natural law. Thus while fire, for example, can be ignited in ways as various as flint and tinder to the roaring outburst which sends a rocket soaring toward the moon, it is nevertheless the same fire and its energy and heat spring immutably from the same combustion.

Emotion, feeling, perception, understanding, are all forms of combustion based upon immutability. There is nothing new under the sun, a wise old sage said once upon a time, thousands of years ago, and this is as true today as it was then. What is here today was always here and always will be here, its form changing but its substance never. It is the substance of which we must learn and which we must accept as permanent truth before we set about changing the form of its expression. Substance is the truth one generation hands on to another and which the new generation must accept if progress is to be made. Scientists know this process very well, for each scientist bases his new discovery upon what another scientist has already learned.

All this is only preamble, perhaps. At least it was in my

mind long before your invitation came. And last week, you remember, when you and a group of your friends were sitting around the fire with me one evening, I tried it out on all of you, to see if I could find out what you would like me to talk about on Commencement Day.

You were all noncommittal, and in the silence I asked a leading question, in order that I might see where your thoughts were. "What do you talk about when you are alone together, without parents or teachers?" I asked.

You looked at each other and then your impetuous redhead friend laughed.

"Sex—sex—sex," she said.

Very well then—sex let it be. For surely sex is an area as wide as life itself, permeating as it does every part of the life of man and woman. Let me be frank—it is also the area in which your generation is experimenting most vigorously, without regard for past knowledge. Why do I say this? Because statistics tell me so. A quarter of a million babies are born out of wedlock each year here in our country. About half of them get adopted; the others drift into orphanages and foundling or foster homes. These children, born displaced, are the result of your experiments with sex.

Yet there is nothing new about sex. All the questions about it have been asked in previous generations, and sex knowledge is as old as life itself. Only the answers are different. In Asia, for example, children are not born out of wedlock. Separation of the sexes at an early age is therefore the answer for most Asian peoples, and arranged marriages a natural consequence. At an age when your

generation is considering whether it is necessary to preserve your virginity, the young Asian is being married in
order to preserve it, so that children may be born only
within the acceptable setting of a family. What Asians
know, what we all know, is that every child has the right
to be born into a family. Security and stability depend
upon a child's being born into a family. Without family no
child grows into a whole human being. This we have
learned, this we know, from one generation to another.

Yet you reject this knowledge when you consider it
possible or even desirable to experiment with sex outside
of marriage. True, you may use contraceptives. Equally
true, they are not reliable or you do not always use them,
else why a quarter of a million children born out of
wedlock every year and orphaned as a consequence?
Virginity may be unimportant in itself, as you say, but
when its loss results in so many lonely, desolate children,
then surely it is important.

You see what I am getting at. I am using sex as an
example of what disaster can come about if one generation rejects the basic knowledge handed on by the preceding one. For there is such a thing as immutable law, the
law of a natural ethic, and the individual cannot break
the natural law without punishment.

A child is a good example of natural law. He is born of
man and woman, of father and mother, as a result of their
sex union. Nothing can change that fact. No experimenta-
tion can change the natural law. When this child is born
according to law, he is not illegitimate. It is the parents
who have behaved lawlessly, although in our society it is

the child who suffers the punishment. Yet I am not sure about this. In her secret heart, the girl mother suffers. She rejects her child, she sends it forth alone among strangers. And perhaps the boy father suffers, too, for he has lost a part of himself. Suffering is punishment.

I know, of course, that you are interested in far more than sex. Yet because sex is of basic concern in the life of men and women together on this earth, I use it now for illustration and illumination. As a woman, you are free today as you have never been free. Old traditions, binding you for centuries, are breaking for you now. Doors are opening for you that until now have been closed. Today, a woman can do anything, can achieve any goal, anywhere. Nothing holds you back, not even the rules and prejudices men once proclaimed. For today men want women to be their friends as well as their lovers; their companions as well as their wives; their comrades as well as their peers.

Man is seeking a new relationship with woman. He is demanding from woman a new equality not only of opportunity but also of performance. This is good, this is welcome, but only if men and women together reach new heights of achievement and happiness. Properly expressed, the cooperation of man and woman will release new creativity in every field of life and art. Selfishly and carelessly expressed, without regard to basic and substantive truth, the new freedom will only bring fresh disorder into our common life.

Yes, sex is, after all, a good example. Its fullest and richest expression, based upon the experience of the human race, results in happy children born into the shelter of family. Its selfish and promiscuous use results in the thousands of displaced children of our times. Be wise, my child!

The world is an old, old place. Each generation is as young as springtime, and yet spring itself follows the laws of birth and growth and death. To know the law and to use it for one's own fullest development—that is the wisdom which alone brings the content we call happiness.

I love you, I who am

Your

Mother

3

My Neighbor's Son

IT IS AUTUMN. The streets of our village and the road at the end of our lane are quiet. The children are back at school, the little ones and the big ones, the first-graders to whom school is a wonder because they know nothing about it, and the high school seniors who know all about it and are already impatiently anticipating the year beyond when they must face the decision of armed services or college or job.

In the houses on the farms and on the streets parents are thoughtful, too. The summer has brought them new acquaintance with their children, and they feel pride, vague alarm, exasperation and hope. Never was there an age so difficult for parents as this age in which we live. We know too well that the world our children face is not the world we faced at their age, and we doubt our ability to help them. They think their parents do not know enough.

It has always been a phase of youth to feel itself misunderstood until maturity brings its own humor and commonsense to dispel the miasma. Yet our children feel more than the pains of growing independence. They conclude, quite simply, that their parents and their teachers do not know enough about our suddenly changed world to warrant faith, and therefore they must discover for themselves what the facts are.

And, aware of this withdrawal, parents read the newspapers and learn of other people's children. They read of boys, not children but young men, who go out to rob and torture and murder innocent and unknown persons. Nor are these the children of bad parents. They may be the sons of respectable, hard-working people who have tried to build good homes and make a decent environment for their children. Their parents cannot believe that the young men, handcuffed and in the custody of the police, are their sons.

"They have always been such good boys!" the parents cry.

"Why didn't you keep them off the streets?" the police retort. "Why didn't you know where your sons were at midnight?"

The parents cannot answer. Anyone who knows teenage boys today, and even teenage girls, knows that it is not easy to insist upon knowing where they are at midnight. Because they do not have faith in their parents they do not respect them. They assert their independence and they think it is part of independence to come and go as they please. What can a middle-aged couple do when a tall, able-bodied son refuses to obey? What are the punishments that can be meted out to a young man by an old

one? The young man sneers at threats; he is contemptuous
of appeal.

"I don't have to take anything from anybody," I heard a
young man shout in the house of the good man who is my
neighbor and his father.

The boy, six feet two, strode out of the house and the
father looked at me.

"What do I do now?" he asked helplessly.

"I don't know," I answered, equally helplessly.

I came home and reflected upon question and answer.
Knowing the father, I felt an unwilling sympathy for the
son; and knowing the son, I felt the same sympathy for
the father. How is it that the son of my neighbor, whom I
first saw when he was a curly-haired baby learning to
walk, has grown into this hooligan? He was an amiable
baby, smiling and friendly. He is not amiable now and he
is not friendly and his smile is usually a sneer. What
happened? His parents are plain, good folk. The mother
has a high school education, the father went to a technical
school and earns a fair salary as a mechanical engineer.
There are two children, a girl in junior high school and a
younger boy. They were smiling babies, too, but they, too,
are not happy children now. Yet their home is pleasant
enough and they have the comforts which today we think
of as necessities. The family goes to church with reasonable regularity, although the children use the church as a
social center rather than as a religious source. The mother
has never worked outside her home. She seldom goes
anywhere, except for her monthly club meeting, and she
is a good cook and housekeeper. The family reads very

little but they like popular music, and they have a television set which occasionally causes strife, for the parents do not enjoy seeing murders and the children do.

It is significant that children today crave scenes of violence. It is because they are angry deep in their souls, so deep that they do not know it. They want to strike back, even vicariously, at a world they fear. Dangerous! Youth, when happy, is in love with life and beauty.

What is wrong in my neighbor's house? Anyone entering it would say that it is a good home. All the furniture and equipment for a good home are there, including parents and children. But when I have stayed there awhile, I have a strange feeling that the house is empty. Nobody is really living there except perhaps the mother in the kitchen.

I wonder why the house feels empty, and after thinking about it, it seems to me that it is because the home is not connected with the stream of life in the community or the nation or the world. It is an island apart, striving to maintain itself in a sea of change. But we human beings need each other, near and far. The separation of the individual or nation or race, whether voluntary or compelled, has dangerous results. We must have constant replenishment from the stream of human life or we thirst and die.

The rebellion of my neighbor's son is inevitable and right. He is rebelling unconsciously and therefore with all his strength against the tomb of his home. He has nothing to do in this house. Oh yes, chores, but why should he work to maintain a tomb? What purpose is there for him in keeping a lawn neat, in weeding vegetable or flower gardens, in washing windows or sweeping out the cellar? They are all parts of the tomb. He has an interest in washing the car and even spending a day or two in simonizing it because there is life in a car. It can take him away from home. Here at home everything is as it has always been as long as he can remember. His father has not changed his mind or his opinions in twenty years, which for the boy is a lifetime. His mother has a flow of talk but no ideas, as far as he is concerned, beyond the cost of food and her longing for a new refrigerator that the father cannot afford. The boy is too young to tap the simple wisdom of his father's philosophy and his mother's compliance. They have discovered that a cup can only hold a cupful. A cup in the kitchen and a cup of life are the same. It contains only so much as it can hold. The parents have settled for what they have. It is a sort of wisdom—call it resignation, if you like.

But the young cannot be resigned unless they have been wounded or deformed. They will not believe that life is no more than a cupful. There must be more somewhere, outside this house. Somewhere there must be joy, peace, security, companionship, understanding, communion. Else why were they born? And the young are right. They, too, have their wisdom.

My neighbor that day watched his tall, strong son climb into the family car and whirl away. I saw despair on his face and bleak helplessness in his eyes.

He said, "We ought to put them all into the Army at sixteen."

I cried out against such defeat. "Oh, don't say that—it means we don't know how to make a world for the young as well as the old."

"I've done all I can," he said, and he turned and went into the house and shut the door.

So the house is really empty and I do not blame the son for leaping into the car and riding away. And yet I know that my neighbor is right when he says that he has done all he can. He faces a task greater than one man can perform.

The whole community must help the parents with their sons and daughters. Schoolteachers must not only teach school, preachers may not only save the souls, police may not merely arrest the criminals, the city fathers may not simply attend to city affairs. They must all help the parents with their children.

In ancient countries, where the social unit is the big family, where grandparents and parents, uncles and aunts and cousins all live together within one surrounding wall and function as a community, the children belong to all. The family community is itself the stream of life, leading into nation and world. But two people struggling to make a living in our highly competitive society in a fluctuating era cannot at the same time feed, clothe, educate, train and inspire a family of restless and lively children.

No two parents have that much strength. And when I say educate, I mean education in the fullest sense, for what teachers have to teach children is very little compared to what parents have to teach children if these parents are conscientious.

In pre-Communist China, for example, the responsibilities of the schoolteacher were much greater than they are here. When parents brought their son to school, they gave him, in a sense, to the teacher. They said, in effect, he is yours not only to teach but to make into a good man. The teachers shared with the parents the responsibility of building character in the pupil. Ancestors, too, helped the parents. Precepts were handed down which all obeyed, young and old, and the son obeyed his dead ancestors as he did his living grandparents and parents.

Had my neighbor lived in old China, scores of people would have helped him with his son, and his son would have felt himself linked to them all and therefore part of the human stream. Instead of this, my neighbor struggles alone with the bewildered help of the boy's mother and the uncertain and intermittent interest of church and school. My sympathies are certainly with my neighbor, for nobody taught him how to be a parent. He spent years learning how to be an engineer. Yet of his two jobs, fatherhood is far more difficult and important than engineering. As for the mother parent, cooking and housekeeping is the least part of being a mother. And nobody helps those parents, not the dead or the living. Yet they are blamed for whatever their son does. In spite of their bewilderment and sense of defeat, they keep on trying.

The boy is wrong, of course, when he is contemptuous of his parents and feels they are useless to him. He has no conception of what heavy hearts they have when they think of him and how much they love him. I do not expect such sensitivity in a boy or girl nowadays. Ours is not a sensitive age. We have been hardened by atrocities. Nevertheless, the son owes it to himself to be courteous and helpful to his parents, regardless of whether he loves them or respects them. When he behaves without courtesy or helpfulness, he is less than fair to himself. But nobody seems to have taught him that. Nor does he know that feeling can follow action or that action must be based on principle and not on feelings.

"Do I have to say I am sorry when I am not?" One of my own sons, when small, made this demand after injustice to his younger sister.

"Indeed you must say you are sorry, and whether you are or not," I replied. "You must *do* right, however you *feel*. You cannot make yourself feel something you do not feel, but you can make yourself do right in spite of your feelings. And you'll be surprised, because when you have learned the habit of saying you are sorry when you should be, you will actually begin to feel sorry."

I learned that precept long ago when I was a child, and my teacher was a wise old man who was not of my race or my religion. I have found it true throughout my life.

And having acted without courtesy or respect toward his father, what satisfaction will my neighbor's son find this afternoon, wherever he is going? He is whirling down the street in a cloud of dust, and my heart goes with him, badly as he has behaved, for I fear he will not find what he really craves, which is to be part of the stream of human life. He will spend the afternoon on the football field and then, with his friends whom he calls "the gang," he will go to the garage, which is today's substitute for the country store or the city saloon, and they will talk about football scores and whether they want to finish high school and what movies they will see and what girls they know and which branch of the service is the easiest and least likely to force them to kill men they have never seen before.

It is a hopeful fact that most of our young people do not want to kill—they still would rather not. I do not believe that those boys I read about in the morning paper, who roamed the city streets, beating and torturing and killing strangers, really wanted to do such things. It is against man's nature to kill his kind. Those boys were pressed beyond endurance by the cruel aspect of the world about them, and in the loneliness of their youth they tried to seize what they thought was life. If someday they must be compelled to violate every natural instinct, then let it be now. They wanted life whatever it had to be. It might as easily have been the saving of lives, if anybody had shown them that in this world, even today, there is the delirious possibility of peace and goodwill.

There was no such conscious reasoning in these tragic boys who, in their ignorance, mistook death for life, but it is unconscious reasoning that we must fear, the despair of the young soul who thinks he cannot escape what he foresees and fears and hates and therefore rushes to meet it. And, looking back, he knows there is no refuge, either, in the life he has lived in the past.

My neighbor's son flees his empty childhood home, but

alas, the football field, the garage, the movie, even the girl he takes out for a few nights and then abandons because she does not satisfy his mind and soul—which do mean more to him, though he does not know it, than his body— these are also empty, for they, too, are not in the main- stream of the world's life.

For I believe that my neighbor's son knows instinctively that there are important and therefore interesting and exciting things to be done in the world, in the nation and even in this home town of his, and he has a vague, blind longing to throw himself into something important and therefore interesting and exciting. His need is the need of the individual to be needed and therefore essential.

How do I know? Once I walked in the evening through the woods at the far end of our farm. I heard the sound of human sobbing, and I stopped to listen. It was a man sobbing, a young man, his voice still breaking. I followed the sound and there, in a small dell, I found my neighbor's son, sitting on a log, his head in his hands. He was crying.

"Are you in trouble?" I asked.

He was startled at the sound of my voice, and he tried to hide his face. "It's nothing," he said. He searched for his handkerchief and, not finding it, he used his shirttail to wipe his eyes.

"Of course it is something," I said, "but I won't ask if you'd rather not talk."

"It's just something personal," he said.

"Troubles are always just personal," I said. "I've had them myself and I know."

I sat down on the far end of the log and waited. It had

been a lovely autumn day; the air was warm, the sky clear, the trees flaming.

"I wouldn't know how to pin it down to one trouble," he said at last. "I just feel pushed around."

"Who pushes you?" I asked. His parents were certainly lenient—permissive is the word.

"Oh, everything . . . sort of . . ."

"You have nothing that you really care about doing," I suggested.

"That's it," he said.

"Or," I suggested, "you haven't found what you really want to do and you don't know where to look."

"I guess so," he said unwillingly.

He looked away from me. "Well, I have to go."

"So do I," I said, getting up from my end of the log. "I just want to say, though, that I hope you won't give up looking for what you really want to do. For I do assure you the world is a wonderful, big place, far beyond your imagination, and there is certainly something in it that you want to do and people who need desperately what you can do. Just keep looking—and be patient with yourself."

"Okay."

He nodded and went off through the woods, and I walked homeward. The very paucity of his speech was a sign of trouble and doubtless added to his frustration. He knew too few words with which to explain himself, and speech is a bottleneck for his surging feelings. "Sort of—". . . . "I guess so—". . . . "Okay!" Such words are the rubber-stamp vocabulary of most of our young people.

But his real suffering is the universal human yearning to belong to something bigger than himself, to be indispensable to his fellowmen, and valued as an individual.

I observe that our American young suffer more deeply than the young of other countries from this conviction of uselessness. Their childhood is prolonged until it becomes a vacuum into which they pour sports, entertainment, jaunting around, "hacking"—all harmless activities but all empty in themselves and none of them substitutes for soul-satisfying work in the mainstream of human life. No one can grow and find content in himself unless he knows that he is contributing his share to the growing, expanding, developing life of the human race.

My neighbor's son has never been taught this deep and simple truth, and so he is lonely and he goes into the woods to weep without knowing why. I hope it is not too late for him to learn. I hope his life will be larger than a cup meagerly filled. Yet he should have begun long ago to learn, when he was still a curly-haired little boy with a smile. We have wasted his youth and strength, as we waste so much of our youth.

Every town and village and city and countryside wastes its young people. Why does so much remain undone? It is because our children have no connection with life. They live in a child world of which they weary and yet which they do not know how to leave. I do not believe in a child world. It is a fantasy world. I believe the child should be taught from the very first that the whole world is his world, that adult and child share one world, that all generations are needed.

If I were the mayor of a town, I would see to it that even first-graders know that they are citizens, and that, as citizens, they have duties. They would be given no privileges but they would have rights. Their very first duties would be essential to the general welfare. They would receive neither pay nor reward for doing their duty, and part of their duty would be to consider how the town could be improved, from their point of view, and their opinions would be given full weight.

If I were the mayor of a town, I would see to it that even a first-grader knows the names of our fine leading citizens, and that he understands what makes men and women good citizens. I would hold the children responsible for part of the care of museums and monuments and public buildings. I would make them realize that it is their duty to cooperate with the police, who are protectors of good people but who in their job as employees of the public must not behave in cruel and tyrannous ways and thus abuse the power which is vested in them by tax-paying citizens.

At each age level the responsibility of the child-citizen should increase. By the time he is twelve, he should understand the government of his town so well that he can assess the character of a man or woman running for public office, because he knows what that person has achieved in character and public service. He should be held responsible for that knowledge by his parents and teachers who, in turn, must furnish him the means of learning. And the child must be given a recognized way of expressing his opinion by a graduated vote.

Had my neighbor's son been part even of the streamlet
of life in his own home town, I do not believe he would
have gone off to weep in the woods because he was lonely.
Responsibility breeds respect, and when our young people
assume responsibility, they deserve our respect. I grieve
to see how little the young are respected in our society.

We love our children and we shower them with privilege, we pamper them with pretty clothes and dashing
cars, we indulge ourselves by being proud of them in a
self-centered sort of way whereby the child is the possession of the parent—"He's my kid, ain't he? So he's none of
your business—" But we do not respect our children as
human beings and individuals. Young Americans, quite
contrary to usual judgment at home and abroad, suffer
almost universally from deep convictions of inferiority.
Their bombastic loudness or their negative withdrawals
are signs of self-doubt. And who can blame them for not
respecting themselves when they are not respected by
society? The respect of one's fellowmen is the source of
self-respect, and for a child it is the primary atmosphere
of growth.

My sympathies are still with my neighbor's son. He has
had very little to help him to grow. His amusements at
eighteen are childish and repetitious or destructive, and
yet they are the only ones to be had. He reads almost
nothing, for he is not really literate, in spite of years of
schooling, and so he does not know that the cream of all
human thought is between the covers of books. Instead,
he looks at comics and those sad funny papers.

I remember once that my mother refused to read a certain magazine, popular in her day, on the grounds that it was only trash. Whether it was trash I do not remember—and it was not important then nor is it now—but what she said was so important that I have never forgotten it.

She said, "I would no more put trash into my mind than I would put garbage into my mouth."

It was her way of expressing an old Biblical wisdom: "As a man thinketh, so he is."

The mind becomes a sewer if it is fed sewage. If, in the name of freedom, we allow the uncontrolled flow of sewage of murder and crime and violence and absurd fantasy to seep continually into the minds of our children, then in the name of freedom we ought to strive with all effort to counteract the flow of evil with a powerful surge of good.

And I deny the sophist who says that good and evil depend upon the person and the standards of his society. Good and evil can be universally defined in their basic essentials, and are so defined by people everywhere. In the many countries in which I have lived and traveled I have been impressed by the discovery that a good human being in one country is considered a good human being in every other. We know instinctively, wherever we were born, what is good and what is evil, but our instincts can become confused.

I think my neighbor's son is confused, and that is part of his trouble. He has been fed on poor fare, mentally and spiritually, and this while his body has been stuffed with good food and vitamins. Little has been expected of him, and he has been limited in his development by that meager expectation.

I do not approve severity but I believe in the inexorable demand for responsibility at each age level of all citizens, and deprivation, if not punishment, when duty is ignored. We need to restore the full meaning of that old word, duty. It is the other side of rights. Each of us has a duty to every human being, and the proper performance of such duty is duty to one's self. Nor is discipline the means to performance. There is a void to be filled in the lives of our young people, and discipline in itself is negative, a prohibition and not a fulfillment.

No, we have to teach our young that they will never find contentment until they put themselves into the mainstream of human life. And then, in the wonderful, rewarding way that life has, peace and happiness—when not sought for their own sakes—come stealing in through the doors of duty fulfilled. Duty is not hateful or tedious or destructive. Duty fulfilled is gratifying and enjoyable and restoring to the soul, and serenity is its fruit.

I pray there is still time for my neighbor's son to know it.

ON LOVE AND MARRIAGE

4

First Meeting

T HE FIRST MEETING between two people, any two people, anywhere, is an occasion. It should not be taken for granted. It must not be entered into carelessly or with boredom, as a chance encounter. Any chance may be the chance of a lifetime. Who knows? There is always the possibility. Avoid, then, the lifted eyebrow, the head half turned away, the limp hand, the suppressed yawn. Avoid even more the falsely cordial voice, the too eager grasp, the aggressive heartiness. All are equally repellent, for all are signs of the self-centered person who seeks and cannot give.

What is the mood, then, for the first meeting? It should be one of mild inquiry. This person I meet for the first time is a stranger to me. But I am also a stranger to the other, man or woman or child. Two strangers, meeting face to face for the first time, must not force themselves upon each other. Each must wait, ready to receive, ready to give. Let naturalness be the approach. I am as I am; the other is as fixed. It is a time for exploration through gentle approach, not a time to rush into smiles too broad or a handclasp too intimate. A firm, cool hand is an encouragement but not a promise.

The eyes, too, must meet. Nothing is so carelessly rude as eyes turned elsewhere while the hands clasp. The eyes must inquire, but calmly. The gaze must not penetrate. A kindly reserve is proper, a pleasant warmth, not individual but conveying simple human friendliness. The length in time of the gaze is important. It should be long enough to be frank but not so long as to be intense. The look thus interchanged should confirm the handclasp but not prolong it.

The voice, meanwhile, must be heard. It must and should be quiet but clear, warm but impersonal. Above all, it should be unhurried. Hands are released, eyes may yield to voice. A natural voice, unhoneyed yet not too casual, is comforting to hear. Let us hope that the nose has nothing to do with the voice, so that the voice may come forth pure from the throat. Silver and not brass is the tone.

What words shall the voice speak? Until now the meeting has been all approach. There has not been direct communication. The moment of speech is the moment of decision. Do we communicate or do we pass each other by? At least let us not use means to announce ourselves. Let neither declare the name of a friend of a friend of a friend of a friend, whom neither knows. What have friends to do with us? Why must one waste time to say that such and such a person is a friend of this other, so that he, the other, must in politeness say, "Oh yes," when perhaps what he longs to say is, "Oh no"? At the first meeting of two, any two, anywhere, let no others exist.

What, then, shall be said? If a greeting, undecorated, is enough, let it be enough. The world is full of people. We cannot meet them all a second time. Best of all is the mere interchange of the two names. Accompanied by the hand-clasp, the look, the voice speaking the two names, completes the meeting. It is enough if there need be no more. Courtesy is accomplished by a slight final smile. But if there is a wish for more, then other words may be spoken. One must not lie now in order to say something, for a lie at first meeting is the most foolish lie of all. It is too obvious. Let only truth be spoken; the first truth that comes to mind will do. It may be of no importance beyond being pleasant.

"When you came in, I was hoping I could meet you."

"Why?"

There must be a truthful reason. Someone has spoken of you to the other. Or the other was lonely in the crowd, and you looked friendly. Or the color of your garment is enchanting. Even, perhaps, your face is unusual. Truth is always exciting. Speak it, then. Life is dull without it. If the truth is unpleasant, it should not, however, be spoken at first meeting. One always has the alternative of the slight final smile before parting.

The first spoken truth is the introduction to conversation. If truth is continued, the conversation will be absorbing because it will reveal. Shall we reveal? Why not? Self-revelation can be on any level one chooses. One should not confide at first meeting but one may reveal, and indeed must reveal, if there is to be a second meeting. If no second meeting is desired, revelation can cease at any point and parting take place.

If there is to be a second meeting, let it not be upon demand. No demands should be made at first meeting. It is too soon. Do not insist upon praise, either to give or to receive. Praise out of season, or tactlessly bestowed, can freeze the heart as much as blame. To praise for the wrong possession or attribute can wound beyond amends. Praise must be given delicately and with full understanding, never extravagantly or without discrimination.

And do not prolong the first meeting, I pray you. It should be short. One must not give too much at first, nor receive too much. Else the two will avoid each other thereafter. "How could I have?" contains the death of a friendship. "Let us meet again" is its promise.

5

Love and Marriage

TWO LADIES from Pakistan sat in my living room. They were guests of the American people, by invitation of the State Department. One was motherly, handsome, and womanwise. The other was young, pretty and sophisticated. Both wore their national costume and both spoke with equal ease in English, French and German. They were traveling over the United States, determined to see everything. Now they were bursting with information, eager with questions, and, being women, they spoke of American love and marriage.

"We feel sorry for American women," the elder of the ladies said cheerfully. She had a lovely voice, rich and warm, and her accent was that of a cultivated English-woman.

"So very sorry," the younger agreed briskly.

"Why should you feel sorry for us?" I inquired, amused.

"American women have so much difficulty with marriage." The rich, warm voice flowed on. "So many divorces, so many girls not able to find husbands!"

"Too much freedom between boys and girls," the

younger voice declared. "Boys and girls learn to despise each other and later they do not marry."

I begged for mercy. "Wait . . . wait . . . it isn't as bad as you think. Most Americans are happily married—by far the most. You don't hear of them because all goes well. It's only the unusual ones, the unhappy ones, who make news."

The ladies rejected this with gestures of exquisite, ringed hands.

"Our Asian way is best," the handsome mother declared. "For example, I have a daughter now ready to be married. She is happy in college, she does not worry about a husband, therefore she can concentrate on her studies. She knows that her father and I will choose several eligible young men. We will bring their names before her and she will decide upon one. Then, if his family is willing, they will meet once or twice. If they are not willing, at least they will allow my daughter to see the young man and he to see her. After due time, the marriage will take place, if all agree together. No, my daughter and the young man are not yet in love, as you Americans say. But they are ready to be in love. They expect to be in love. And the marriage will also be based on solid family approval after the four parents have met and discussed everything together."

The younger lady hastened to agree. "For example, I am responsible for the marriage of my younger brother because my parents are dead. I am myself a happily married woman. My parents chose my husband for me when I was twenty, and we have three children now. As the sister of my brother, I have to choose a wife for my brother. He wishes me to do so."

"I don't believe American parents would like such responsibility," I observed. "We'd be afraid we might make a mistake and then our children would blame us."

"My brother will never blame me," the lady declared. "He is sure I will do my best for him and that I know better than he does what woman will suit him."

"Our marriages are happier than yours," the handsome mother added. "And our women are happier."

"You have not seen enough of our American women," I insisted. "Most of us are happy."

We defended our positions stoutly but with good humor—they, the Asians, and I, the American—and we parted an hour or two later with concessions on both sides.

"In spite of your freedoms and your technical machines," the elder lady said as we bade each other good-bye, "it remains true everywhere in the world that good relationship between man and woman is the foundation of happiness, and this relationship is basically marriage and love."

"We would put it love and marriage," I reminded her.

"Aha," she said, with a flash of her fantastically beautiful eyes. "Who is right?"

"We agree at least upon this point," I said. "Marriage is the most important experience for man and woman, whether in Asia or America."

They were gone, and ever since I have thought about what they said. Is their judgment of American men and

women a just one? Are we to be pitied or are we to be
envied? Are we happy or unhappy? We are individuals, of
course, but granting individualism, are there problems
and difficulties peculiar to the American husband and
wife? Does the nearly complete freedom we have destroy
the web of mystery and romance which we still demand
in the love relationship? Is it true, as I have heard it said,
that American women have become too aggressive and
that men are in retreat and rebellion?

"American marriage is in real trouble today," a young
American husband wrote me a few weeks ago. I think I'd
put it, instead, that men and women feel the need of new
and mutual understanding. They are trying to achieve a
new unity in an ancient institution. In other countries and
other times, marriage has been a convenience, a necessity
for economic and family, as well as personal, reasons. In
our country and in our age, at least the economic reasons
for marriage are disappearing. Men and women separately can now earn good livings, can make houses into
pleasant homes. Women need not be family cooks and
housekeepers, and men need not be family breadwinners,
unless they wish it. Marriage today is increasingly for
individual satisfaction, companionship and love, and for
the chosen joys of children and family. The old ideas of
heirdom and carrying on a clan name, so motivating in
Asia, have all but ceased to exist in our country. Personal
fulfillment through union in the highest and most complete sense is what we hope for in marriage. It is a manifold hope, and to realize it requires equal effort from man
and woman.

I realize that I an influenced by my own American marriage to believe that a good marriage is the natural source of happiness for both man and woman. I admire men and women who build fine, fruitful lives without marriage, but perhaps they would have been better still, because happier, if they had had the experience of good marriage. Yet nothing is more dreadful, more stultifying, more defeating than an unhappy marriage. It degrades both man and woman and there should be a decent and legitimate escape from it. But a good marriage!

Well, what is a good marriage?

Let me choose one I know well, by way of illustration. Mary and Robert, my neighbors and friends, married young but not too young. That is, they were old enough to recognize each other as individuals and not as mere symbols of romance, and yet they were romantic enough to be deeply in love. Both of them come from families of about the same social status and income. Neither is extraordinary in looks, but they are good-looking and healthy. They like the same things to a comfortable degree and enjoy the same pastimes: Robert plays tennis and Mary is good at golf. They both prefer country to city, but they were able to enjoy the city until their income was enough to live elsewhere. They disagree mildly on various points but are fundamentally alike in their tastes and standards and they laugh at the same jokes. They travel occasionally but they are essentially home-loving. They are both affectionate, and I suspect passionate, and they believe in expressing their feelings to each other and to their four children in words and actions. All this adds up to saying that the marriage is good because the two, man and woman, are, generally speaking, of the same temperament and background and neither has had to give up very much, and there has been little of strain and argument in their relationship. They are fond of saying that they like as well as love each other.

It is difficult to make a good marriage between persons of opposite temperaments, backgrounds and education. Mary and Robert have adjusted comfortably but have remained essentially themselves because they are basically alike. This does not mean that they always do the same things. Mary is an accomplished musician, for example, and Rob does not care much for music. But Mary is not afraid to continue with her music, and Rob is proud of her playing. They have pleasant dispositions and they never belittle each other. It would not occur to them to do so. A commonplace couple? Yes, perhaps, but both are commonplace to about the same degree, and neither feels inferior to the other. There is nothing to destroy love between them.

A good marriage is one where love is not destroyed. Love changes, of course, in its manifestation as time goes on and as individuals achieve higher levels of maturity, but change does not mean destruction. It can and should mean growth. A good marriage is one which allows for change and growth in the individuals and in the way they express their love.

I confess that when Mary and Rob were married, twenty-five years ago, they were almost embarrassing in their obvious love. Today, love pervades their relationship in the frankness of their conversation, in the quiet looks exchanged, in their mutual and unconscious deference, but they no longer need to hold hands or even to kiss in public. They approve each other, and mutual approval is the earth from which love blooms eternal. Mary and Robert chose each other in youth and they still choose each other.

The ladies from Pakistan may be right, but Asia's ways are not ours. True, I see Asia's advantages. There are American women who have no opportunity for marriage.

I said only yesterday to a pleasant elderly woman in my neighborhood, "Sally, it is none of my business but why have you never married? You are so lovable."

To which she answered with equal frankness, "I have only had one proposal in all my life and it was from a human worm whom no self-respecting woman would marry."

I would not have believed her except that I observe the adolescent males in my immediate vicinity and their habit of pursuing *en masse* our prettiest girls and ignoring the other girls until the beauties make their choice. Our American way of marriage is not always fair to women, and yet I daresay men are disappointed as often as women. Even Sally's human worm has made so many efforts to get a wife that he is a local joke, poor fellow!

Competition is our law, even in marriage, and in any competition the wholly successful are few. But few, too, are the wholly defeated. Most of us, men and women, must settle for what we can get. How cheerfully we settle decides for or against our happiness in love and marriage, as it does in the rest of life, and that most people wish to marry and do marry proves that marriage is still fundamentally and equally the most important experience for men and women.

Granted then that marriage is a blessed state, how can a man and woman build a good marriage together? Granted, too, is the fact that they honestly hope to make each other happy and that neither wishes to dominate the other or limit personal freedom.

I was convinced again of this fact when, not long ago, I sat with a group of intelligent young professional men and listened to their concern about women. Since they were all married and all had young children, they talked in terms of personal experience, and I was impressed by their genuine love for their wives and their anxiety that their wives be happy, not only in family life but as human individuals. Their only question was, What did their wives want and how could what they want be provided within the framework of modern marriage and home and the necessity for man, at least while the children were young, to be the chief provider of funds?

Personal happiness included the consideration, too, of sexual compatibility. The young husbands spoke frankly of their own responsibility in this aspect of marriage. Until rather recently, it has been taken for granted that the sexual satisfaction of the male in marriage has been the only necessity, since, it was thought, woman's satisfaction was chiefly in motherhood. These young husbands were patently concerned over the modern idea that woman also has personal sexual needs and that it is man's responsibility to see that she is satisfied.

One young man, in sudden distraction, cried out: "What with all this sex education in schools and books, the average man is afraid to get married! Why, the very idea that he is responsible for the woman's fulfillment is enough to make him impotent!"

The laughter that followed this outburst was laced, I felt, with ruefulness. Sex in woman is a subtlety unless she has been debased. And doubtless a husband did find marriage easier in the nineteenth century when a "decent" woman kept her sex needs, if any, to herself. In those days a man could think comfortably only of himself.

There can be no return, however, to the past, and while men and women may be alike in their longing for complete fulfillment in love and marriage, they are nevertheless different in their approach to such fulfillment. Men must know that, and women must tell them. I can best express the difference by saying that man's approach is physical, but for woman it is not physical. For her the physical is consummation.

My sensible neighbor put it very well the other day when I was discussing this article with her. She said, "I know that when my good old Fred sees a pretty girl his first instinct is to wonder how she would be in bed. Now I don't think that's a sin—he can't help it and the girl probably takes it as a compliment. But when I see a good-looking man, I wonder first what sort of a person he is. Maybe I'll get to the bed idea later—I don't say it isn't possible—but if he doesn't interest me first as a person, I'll never get to it. And you'd be surprised how seldom I do—maybe really never. I'm a little on the subtle side, I guess."

She is right. Her femaleness is subtle and inherent in her whole nature; it permeates her being and her mental processes. I do not wonder at a young husband's concern. Time, effort and even some intelligence are required in order to comprehend his wife completely and certainly if he loves her.

It must be remembered, too, as an added problem of modern marriage, that our modern life is deeply influenced by wars and military life. Many men, as a consequence, have learned to enjoy only a simple and even crude approach to women. Indeed, it is doubtful whether women or men realize fully how much militarism affects their secret personal lives.

To take but one example: when males are segregated into armies at a young age—before they have had time to become fixed in heterosexual patterns—it is inevitable and historically proven that there is great increase in homosexuality. Though this trait may not express itself overtly, and indeed usually does not, yet for some men the homosexual image predominates in love relationships long after their enforced segregation is over, and causes untold sorrow to their wives as well as to themselves. And even though we are not in actual war, the military draft does the same damage, for it enforces the same separation from normal female companionship at a critical pattern-forming age.

This abnormal pattern expresses itself in other ways, too, curious and interesting. In a military age, for example, men may unconsciously prefer women to look boyish. Thus we see women slim themselves down into boylike figures, cut their hair short, wear men's shirts and man-tailored suits and slacks and dungarees, use the vocabulary of boys, swear easily, cultivate four-letter words, and generally shed femininity. It is an unconscious process but nonetheless actual. In times of prolonged peace, on the other hand—especially when males are no longer drafted and the fear of wars has passed—the sexes again tend to assume their proper aspects, the men become masculine, the women feminine.

Nor is it latent male homosexuality alone that tends to produce mannish women. While men are away at camp or at war, their responsibilities are thrust upon women. Woman has to be father as well as mother. She learns to do man's work, not because she likes to but because she must. She tries to do it as well as she can and takes a natural pride in her performance. And the man, for his part, becomes accustomed to irresponsibility in his over-protected military life. He is isolated from competition, from the struggle of earning even his own food, clothing and shelter. Everything is provided for him while he goes through the gymnastics of preparing for battle. In battle, he may face death itself but these are brief moments, fatal or not, and the total result of military life is to remove man from the practical world of everyday life.

When he comes home, he is at a loss, certainly temporarily. All the protection is gone and he faces responsibility again. It is a tremendous adjustment for him and he may never make it successfully. Meanwhile his wife, in his absence, has been forced to learn his role, and perhaps all too well, and does not know how to give it up.

The adjustment is difficult for both. Husband blames wife for being aggressive, even unfeminine. Where, he wonders, is the gentle, yielding creature he left behind him? He cannot recognize her in this competent, strong woman he finds his wife. And she? She has found a new self in her own competence. She knows she is using her abilities as she never did before. It is only human to love power, yet I believe that women rarely love power for its own sake. She enjoys power because, with it, she can get things done for her family. And because she likes her new self, she tries to keep it, believing that she is now functioning fully as a woman.

A pretty young wife, discussing this with me the other day, flung out her angry defense: "We're always hearing about women unmanning men. Well, men unwoman us!"

"What do you mean by that?" I asked.

She tossed back her long, blond hair. "I mean that I don't believe in a woman's subjecting herself to man, any more than I believe in a man letting himself be bossed by a woman. I want to be myself, full and free and not called aggressive and unwomanly for it. Tom ought to realize that when I'm being myself I'm being most really a woman. And when he tries to put me down and make me feel inferior again, he unwomans me!"

Well, Tom must realize somehow that Julie is not superior or inferior to him. Brain capacity, the ability and the talent, varies not with the sex but with the individual, for the laws of inheritance are impartial. The genius of a brilliant father is as likely to appear again in a daughter or granddaughter as in son or grandson. The power to think and to create exists in equal degree in man and woman and they must respect each other equally as human beings if they are to be happy in marriage.

And while we are speaking of creative genius, equally inherited, here let me pause to say that as a woman and a wife I do not accept the hackneyed statement, traditionally expressed by certain types of men, that woman has not created and therefore cannot create great works of art. She is the creator in the most basic sense.

Consider, for example, how she receives into herself a bit of chemical material and from it creates a human being. It may be asked, Is even this bit of chemical material essential? Science whispers already that it is not. Years ago a scientist fertilized a rabbit's ovum with a simple assortment of chemicals from a test tube. He then transplanted the ovum into the uterus of a female rabbit, and the baby rabbit developed normally and was born without benefit of father. It can be done, but let us pray that science halts with the rabbit. For his own happiness, man must remain essential and therefore for woman's happiness. Happiness must be mutual for man and woman or it becomes unhappiness.

And, furthermore, if woman has not as yet risen to frequent preeminence in the creative arts, may it not be because she has been limited to a sphere? The first necessity for artistic creation is, surely, the free mind, the unhampered hands, and woman has not been free in either hand or mind. Indeed, so long has she been told that she is inferior to man that she herself has come to think that she must be his inferior, and so, like a slave, to accept, humbly or angrily, the narrow space allotted to her.

Mozart's sister was known to be more talented than he was, but their father would not allow her to continue her musical education lest it take her beyond her "sphere." She submitted, trained in submission, just as Chinese women in the not distant past themselves bound their daughters' feet even as their own feet had been bound, in spite of the pain and the crippling, and thought they were doing their duty.

In the slave labor that built the Great Wall of China, that dug the Suez Canal, that works in the camps of Communism today, doubtless there were and are even men with high talent and some with genius who nevertheless have remained and will remain lost to the human race because they could not and cannot fulfill their potentialities under the circumstances in which they were and are compelled to live. In the same way, among women, there have been many talented and some of genius, in numbers proportionate to males, who, like slaves, were not merely lost in the traditional tasks of home and childbearing, but were excluded by tradition from opportunities open only to men.

Men have become accustomed to thinking of women as limited to a sphere, and it may be alarming to them, especially if they be the timid sort, when women begin, as they are now doing, to emerge from the traditional sphere. It takes a brave man to face a brave woman, and man's fear of woman's creative energy has never found an expression more clear than in the old German clamor, renewed by the Nazis, of *"Kinder, Kuchen* and *Kirche"* for women.

To my astonishment, I hear its reverberations sometimes in our own country. Even certain male psychiatrists, who ought to know better, are saying that women are discontented because their "sphere" is not defined. Better, these men say, that we return to the "certainties" of the nineteenth century. Yet anyone who has read and studied the books of the nineteenth century without bias must realize that, while men may have been happy in an adolescent sort of way when women had a limited "sphere," the nineteenth century was bitterly unhappy for women and cannot therefore have been really happy for mature men. Indeed, the discontents that were expressed through feminism had their root source in the injustices of woman's life in the nineteenth century, and the primary injustice was that she was first denied the opportunity of choosing her sphere, and second, the right to share in policy decisions.

Today, women may choose their sphere, even though they be wives, for the modern trend is for husband and wife to accept equal responsibility in home life except perhaps for a few necessary years when the wife is bearing children. This is good, but not good enough, for women are still far from having an equal voice with men in the policy-making centers of community life, national and international, in spite of comparable education and skills. This right, women, of course, must and will assert for themselves, for it is the final and most important step in their progress toward a full companionship with men, based on mutual freedom and shared responsibility at home and in the world.

A wise husband will help and encourage his wife toward the step, for he knows that the mass discontent of women—the result of having little or no voice in shaping a better world—can seep even into the marriage relationship and poison it. For it is inevitable that an intelligent woman, realizing the inability of women to contribute to the conduct of human affairs, will unconsciously turn peevish at times even toward her own loved husband, merely because he symbolizes the male in control of an unsatisfactory world. No true mother ever sent a son off to war without believing in her heart that had she a voice in the world's affairs there would be no wars; and if she gets, one day, the announcement of his death, she knows, though she be silent, that the sacrifice need not have been.

And why, woman asks, may she not share in shaping world life? Why else, she answers, except that man wants his own way and fears her power to defeat him? He is afraid of her and she knows it when he uses force, physical or mental, to limit her to a "sphere." Crude force may make woman temporarily subject, but it never wins her respect or her love. The notion of a caveman dragging a smiling female by the hair to his cave is pure male fantasy—a wistful dream that never was or will be reality. Man's fear may not be overtly expressed, but it is revealed in the common "he-man" delusion that women crave rough treatment and enjoy being forced into bed or sleeping bag. Such male timidity enrages woman, and her anger compels her to a further aggressiveness which she actually hates in herself because it is against her nature.

I was visited the other day by a strong, brilliant woman of middle age, and she was a whirlwind of fury.

"What's wrong?" I demanded when she could get her breath.

She burst into tears. "I've been beastly to Hal again," she sobbed. "Simply beastly! I hate myself. But how dare he give in to me so? How can I keep on loving him? And I want to keep on loving him—"

"You'd better stop being just a home woman," I said. "You need to get out of the house."

It is true. She is a woman with far too much capacity, and no house can contain her. She adores her children but for their sakes, too, she needs to get out of her sphere. For the sake of a conscience trained by tradition, she denies herself the opportunities she longs to accept and punishes those she loves. In this modern day she is trying to live in the past. It cannot be done.

Yet Hal is not to be blamed altogether. Man's fear of woman is founded deeply in racial experience. For, as we consider the causes of marital discontent we cannot escape the fact that husbands and wives are first men and women, and the history of male and female has its own vast epochs.

In the beginning, women were the race and man's part in conception was not known. That was the age of matri-

archy when women believed that the children they bore
were the result of divine conception, the messengers of
such divine begetting the birds, or later "angels," winged
creatures that came down from the skies. The ancient
belief still lingers in the myths of many peoples, in the
stork that "brings the babies," in the doves descending
from heaven, and so on.

Primitive women, gathering together for the protection
of themselves and their children, developed cities and
built temples and created the arts. They were the rulers
and man was subject. Not until his part in conception was
first guessed at and then declared, was he able to rise to
equality with woman; and then, by physical strength and
freedom from responsibility, to wrest from her the ruling
powers of church and government. The story of the final
defeat of woman by man and the rise of man as father,
only proved scientifically as late as 1875 by a German
scientist, Von Hertwig, makes fascinating reading and
gives food for fruitful reflection. We are still in the age of
man's supremacy, this patriarchal age. Meanwhile, forgotten memories hide in man's brain cells and, unconscious though he be of their existence, make him still
fearful of woman and reluctant to allow her a place equal
to his own in the power centers.

And to the old subconscious memories of an age when
woman was supreme, the conditions of our modern life
add their own burden to man. Women are the discipli-
narians in the modern home and are perforce the constant
naggers if not the final authority. It is natural for a father
to avoid conflicts with his children in the brief hours

while he is at home. Perhaps, too, certain men, less mature than others, still instinctively feel that the children belong primarily to the mothers. This is understandable. It is easy to beget a child. It can be done without thought and with little or no emotion. But to conceive a child is another matter, and to live in closest communion and alone with an unborn child for nine months is an intimacy so profound and formidable that it may indeed raise a barrier between husband and wife.

Then, too, women must continue the discipline in school, since most teachers are still women, and thus man carries the rebellions of childhood into his adulthood, and his rebellion against mother and teacher may develop into rebellion, secret or overt, against wife. And she, alas, too often continues beyond the wedding day her role as disciplinarian and is forlorn and bewildered when she divines that love is gutted by fear.

For woman, by her very nature, must admire and respect before she can love, and man has too often put on only the show of strength and wisdom. Then woman, thus deceived, turns bitter, and the bitterest creature under heaven is the wife who discovers that her husband's bravery is only bravado, that his strength is only a uniform, that his power is but a gun in the hands of a fool. She turns cold with bitterness and she resigns from life, and when she resigns from life she merely goes through the motions of day and night. When a man complains that his wife has ceased to take an interest in life, that the marriage has become dull, I know that his wife is not only resigned in spirit but has actually resigned from their marriage. Ah yes, there was a death struggle before she gave up. She was probably nagging and domineering and not very pleasant to live with; people who face death usually put up a struggle of a sort not pleasant to see. And when a woman gives up in marriage and becomes merely a house automaton, she usually gives up in the community, too, and so society loses her and all her gifts.

It is, of course, not always the wife who gives up. Some women die less easily than others. They persist in struggling against death, and in the struggle it may be the husband who yields first. He may become the automaton, and the more helpless he is—the more obedient to her self-protecting anger against him for his yielding—the more agonized the wife is, and her agony may take the tragic form of harsh criticism and bitter scorn. Who has not seen love dying between husband and wife under the lash of mirthless laughter and sarcastic humor! These are the weapons a woman uses in self-torture against the man she cannot love. For she yearns to respect her husband in order to love him with her whole heart and her whole mind—yes, and with her body, too, for it is only when a wife loves her husband with mind and heart that she can love him also with her body. And it is basic for happiness in the human family that woman be able to love man physically.

Contrary to superficial public opinion, and even, I am shocked to observe, superficial expert opinion, wives do not want to "mother" their husbands. The concept of "Momism" is male nonsense. It is the refuge of a man seeking excuses for his own lack of virility. I have listened to many women in various countries, and I have never found a woman who willingly "mothers" her husband. The very idea is repulsive to her. She wants to mother the children while they are young, but never their fathers. True, she may be forced into the role of mother by a man's weaknesses and childishness, and then she accepts the role with dignity and patience, or with anger and impatience, but always with a secret, profound sadness unexpressed and inexpressible.

I hear my own countrywomen say sometimes, and too many times, "Oh well—you know how men are. They never grow up." The words may be uttered with apologetic laughter and seeming good nature, but they do not conceal the hidden sadness. Every wife longs to love her husband with respect and admiration. She longs, above all, to love him with utter confidence in his mature integrity.

I do not speak for woman alone. For man, too, is deprived of ultimate happiness when woman does not love him wholly. And one-sided love is impossible, for ultimately love dies without full response. Love must feed upon love. When, therefore, a wife resigns and is resigned, she gradually ceases to love and therefore to respond, and so, by that very resignation, she dooms herself. When she no longer believes in her husband as a man, he begins to be afraid of her and in turn he ceases to love her.

Happily, however, two generations of enlightened education are beginning to tell in the minds and behavior of both men and women in the United States. While we have exceptions in both sexes, most of us are coming to realize that husbands and wives are equally responsible for the success of marriage, or to put it in a word, their own happiness. This is the beginning of wisdom.

Yet every husband and wife must remember that their marriage is not a thing apart from human history or even from the present moment in history. Wives must know the fears that husbands may have as men, and husbands must understand the restiveness of wives as women. A wife has the duty of winning the confidence of her husband so completely as a person whom he need not fear that, whatever her position may be—whether as chauffeur in the home or as President in the White House—he is willing to accept all women. And the husband must recognize the fact that sudden and inexplicable changes of mood and temper in his wife may not be because of him, individually, but because she has in some way been forced to realize again that men in general do not as yet accept women as human beings on a level with themselves. And so she, his wife, unconsciously vents on him, her husband and the man closest to her, the vexation she feels. He must be patient at such times, and quick to realize that women are struggling, consciously and unconsciously, to arrive at the time when they can claim their place, even in the policy-making centers of the world.

For, inevitably, woman will refuse, one of these days, to carry out decisions made by man alone. Inheriting intelligence equally with man and having always her own special talents in intuition and in practical human relations, she knows that she has gifts which thus far she has had no opportunity to contribute to human welfare. The knowledge is compelling her to action. If a husband does not fear his wife as a woman, he will be glad that she is ready to share with him the heavy responsibility of the world.

I believe that as man ceases to fear woman, woman will gain in respect for man. She does not any longer, as she did in the days when she needed brawny slaves, admire the hairy chest, the monstrous shoulders, the big muscles and the small brain cap. Today she admires the healthy male who is intelligent and self-controlled, who is mature enough to realize that she is a human being, not subject to him—and wise enough not to want her to be subject—because life is at its best for man only when woman is her true self. And woman can be her true self only when she is free and is encouraged by man to exercise her freedom fully.

What is a wife's chief responsibility today?

It is to prove to her husband, and through him to all men, that he need never fear her as she moves toward that complete equality with him in life which alone can bring happiness for them both.

And what is the husband's responsibility?

It is to encourage and help his wife, and through her all women, to be her free self, and so to release her talents for the world as well as the home.

When these mutual responsibilities are fulfilled, American marriages will, I believe, be even more rewarding than they are now.

6

The New Marriage

T HERE IS nothing new about marriage," John said.
John is a friend of many years, the solid, conservative son of a radical, independent father. He and his wife
Mary and their newly married young daughter Joan and
her husband Mark sat in my living room. John is a fine
man, intelligent and forthright. His work takes him
around the world at least once a year, and now that Joan
is married, Mary goes with him. We meet with mutual
eagerness to discuss everything that is happening everywhere.

I had just put the question to which John had made
answer. I turned to Mark. "Do you agree? Or is it too soon
to ask?"

"I don't agree," he said positively, "and it's not too soon
to ask. Joan and I talked about this long ago."

"What do you want out of marriage that you think your
parents didn't have?" I asked.

Mark is a thoughtful young man, intellectual in his
tastes, highly educated, still in his early twenties. Of
course Joan is an unusual girl. She has traveled with her

parents, she speaks several languages very well, she is a college graduate.

"I want companionship," Mark said. "And when I say companionship, I mean I want a real companionship, not just a good housekeeper and a mother for my children. I expect to spend the rest of my life with Joan, and I want to be able to talk with her about everything that interests me. I don't want to have to explain things to her. I want her to know what I mean when I talk about the diffusion of neutrons, for example."

I turned to Joan. She is a pretty girl, rather quiet, and she sat beside Mark, saying nothing and smiling.

"Is that a tall order, Joan?"

She shook her head. "I know what he means."

"I wouldn't have married her if she didn't," Mark said.

I persisted. "And you, Mark—do you understand everything she may want to talk about?"

"We're interested in the same things," he said. "I took care of that. I made up my mind long ago that when I married it would be to a girl in my own field. There's no time nowadays to build long bridges across the chasms between man and woman. If she hadn't wanted to marry a man in her field, then she wouldn't have married me. I'm in her field as much as she's in mine."

He turned to John. "That's what's new in marriage, sir. We're beginning our marriage at the point the older generation reached after years of mutual love and effort. We're ready to live together."

John shifted the conversation. "Let's talk about politics!"

After they were gone, I went back to Mark's answer to

my question. Is he right? Is this demand something new in marriage? What do men and women expect of one another when they marry? I suppose, now as always, they expect, or hope for, the satisfaction of their needs. The needs, again in general terms, have always been the same —security and belonging, love, companionship on some level, home and children. But there is something new in this word *companionship,* which Mark stressed with peculiar emphasis.

Mark is a very modern young man. He has been educated in specific fields and he wants a new kind of companionship—the sort of companionship which heretofore men have usually expected only from other men. He wants it now from his wife. Does this mean he cares less about the other needs? Knowing many young men among family and friends, I should say no, he does not care less about the other needs, but he believes they will follow the companionship. He may be right. Sexual satisfaction, simply speaking, is not as difficult to secure as it once was. In other generations, a normally fastidious man might include love as a necessary preliminary to sex, and sex might therefore be a strong compulsive force toward marriage. This is much less true today than it was a generation ago.

I can express it succinctly by quoting what a young man said the other day in New York: "The number of available women in this city puts a strain upon men."

I am compelled to conclude that many women no longer have the standards in sex matters that they once had. This may be good or bad for society eventually—I don't know. But it does mean that fulfillment of physical sex is found as often outside of marriage as within. As long as it is not announced, woman lives as she pleases today—or may so live.

For what, then, does a man marry nowadays? Not necessarily for home! The number of cheerful young bachelors I know, living in pleasant apartments or houses of their own, either individually or in groups, and their excellence in housekeeping matters, with or without servants, gives food for female thought. Nor do they lack the woman's touch. They are surrounded by adoring and wistfully hopeful young women always ready to play hostess or traveling companion or even wife. If the young men want children, they keep the wish to themselves. I hear no hint of longings for fatherhood. They are too busy with their jobs and their careers. They are wary of marriage, although they say they want to marry eventually, if and when they find that impossible perfect woman. Probably most of them will marry before they grow old, and many of them will marry several times. In short, they do not rule out marriage. They are not homosexuals— there are always women available, and women of their own class and kind—but they will marry only when they find the women who fulfill their exacting requirements.

In contrast, there are also the very young marriages, boys and girls who marry and begin life together soon after high school. We do not yet know what will happen to these marriages. I shall only quote a few figures from a study made in recent years by one of our great universities. The subject for study was modern American woman. It was disclosed that the average American woman of today gets engaged at the age of nineteen. She marries at twenty-one, and by the time she is twenty-six she has all her children, the number being three. By the time she is thirty-one, all her children are in school at least part of the day, she lives in a small but well-equipped house, and she has forty-four years to live. Forty-four years, with the mental equipment of a girl of nineteen! Her husband will continue to grow, but unless she is helped, she probably will not grow. Companionship is impossible unless she realizes her plight and does something about it.

So, is there something new about marriage today? Yes, there is. What's new is the demand of modern man for a different kind of woman. The modern young man, as I know him, no longer wants a girl like Mother. Mother was all very well in her place but he wants a wife, a woman whose mind matches his own in intelligence, curiosity, capacity for growth, interest in life at home and in the world at large. He wants companionship on a scale and to a degree and of a quality which he has not had. He is not attracted to the beauty parlor product. He is contemptuous of the "tired businessman." He will never be one of those. And he is profoundly impatient of women and often deeply angry with them. Why don't women grow up, he growls, not realizing that his new demand is a sign of his own very recent and still incomplete maturity.

This impatience and secret anger color all his relationships with women, at home and elsewhere, but he keeps his feelings to himself because he is kind, because he likes women, because he yearns for a woman with whom he can really communicate. He searches for her, of course, and is often disappointed. Then he is unjust and may conclude that women are hopeless. He is extremely wary of the woman who angles for him with the lures of sex. That she can think he is so naïve in this day and age when sex is spread on every page and billboard and waits at every corner, deepens his secret contempt for women. Sex—yes! Marriage—no, not until . . . and he continues the search.

What about women? Sometimes I think that women have not yet recovered from the discovery that men are indispensable to them. The shock destroyed their primeval self-confidence, and they have not yet found a way to regain it. Woman, in early times, was the ruler, the priestess, for she and man believed that she alone conceived and bore the child. Here was the brain that began first to wonder and thus to grow. Whence came this power of creation within herself?

Centuries passed before either woman or man understood that man has his essential part in creating new life. When he first suspected it, no one knows. Nor is it known what brilliant male brain first put two and two together, sexual union and birth of a third, and so roused the first suspicion. When it was suspected, however, man asserted his paternity. He then demanded exclusive possession of woman, and women, hitherto available to any man, were segregated into private places, each by one man, so that her children were his. Matriarchy became patriarchy.

We are still living in this second stage in most of the world. There are signs, however, that this stage, too, is drawing to a close, and this because the most modern man is thinking of woman as he never has before. He is thinking of woman as companion, first of all—a companion to him on equal terms as a human being, not merely as the mother of his children and keeper of his house. This puts a new demand upon woman, a demand that is both challenge and opportunity which, if she accepts, will give her, or so I believe, a happiness that she has never yet known.

Will she accept the challenge? Will she seize the opportunity? Ah, that is the question! The long centuries of shelter in the house, the local tasks of cooking and cleaning and caring for children, the easily fulfilled demands of a simple physical sex which she can give without effort or even sharing, are no longer enough for man. This man, this modern man, wants her whole self; he demands that she be herself at full growth, his mate in every sense and perception.

It is far more than has ever been asked of her before. What will she do? She has exhausted all her little sex tricks. There are too many pretty girls everywhere, younger and younger, so that the years of a girl's prettiness are few indeed. By the time she is twenty-five she is already too old to be merely a pretty girl. There must be more to her than that. In her panic, she tries to marry before she is out of her own childhood and long before she is a woman. She burdens herself with household cares and children before she is old enough to manage them, and she robs herself and the man of what she could have been had she given herself time to grow, had she been willing to complete herself, enrich her mind with knowledge and her emotions with the depth of maturity. In her panic, too often, she bestows her little sex wares upon some boy or man, even without the assurance of marriage, and thereby makes it harder perhaps for any women to marry.

"Why buy a cow?" a farmer's crude son said the other day, "when you can get the milk free?"

Woman is in a predicament in our modern world. Man is no longer holding her back. He is urging her on. The day of our grandmothers, and even our mothers, is over. There is nothing for women to rebel against, and many of them are frightened and trying to find shelter and excuse in being "just a housewife." The responsibility is terrifying now that they can be whatever they wish to be. Will they face the fact that men want women to be their fullest and best selves as human beings? If they are willing, then the rewards are rich indeed. But they must help themselves and one another.

That nineteen-year-old girl who has forty-four years to live after she is thirty-one must be given better equipment than a nineteen-year-old brain. She must have the opportunity for more schooling after thirty-one if not before. Who will take care of the children? Who will clean the house? These tasks are easy when the brain is equipped. Once the *what* is decided, the *how* always follows. We must not make the *how* an excuse for not facing and accepting the *what*.

Women must help each other, first of all, by believing in themselves. Then they will believe in and help one another. Whenever, for example, I hear a woman say she trusts a doctor because he is a man rather than a woman, I know that here is a woman who has a low opinion of herself. Otherwise she would choose the best doctor she could find, man or woman. A woman, to put it bluntly, is against other women because she fears she herself is inferior. Yet if she stopped to reason, she would realize that nature knows no sex limitations and does not bestow brains upon men alone. Daughters inherit gifts exactly as often and as much as sons.

Well, you may say, women do a great deal. Yes, the small jobs of a community are usually performed by women, and women are very busy with these small jobs, but where are women in the policy-making centers? Were women sitting there with men, many of these small community jobs, the result of poverty and bad administration and ill-balance, might not be necessary at all. For centuries, religious and other groups have worked at care for the poor, the sick and war-wounded, but these same groups do nothing, or very little, to prevent the frictions which result in war and disease and poverty. The world, now so closely knit into one community, needs whole thinking at top levels—that is, thinking men and women. Women are not at top levels. It is self-deceptive to say that men do not want them there. Men do want them there if they are wise, informed human beings, ready to apply themselves to the tasks ahead.

There *is* something new in marriage. Man is making

new demands on woman. He wants a new kind of woman for a wife.

Perhaps, if she accepts the challenge and the opportunity, she may have a few demands of her own to make on him. He is not perfect, this man. But he is asking woman now to be perfect. It is the first step toward mutual growth. Women have always wanted to be what men want them to be, and though they are not so blatant about it, men want to be what women want them to be. If woman now takes the first step toward man, in faith, then marriage will be better than it has ever been—a closer companionship on every level, a happiness beyond previous experience. Nothing in life is as good as the marriage of true minds between man and woman. As good? It is life itself.

7

When a Daughter Marries

I AM AN American parent, but there are aspects of my position that I dread. Our children are growing up so fast that I know the hour is not far off when one by one they will all find mates and marry. I welcome it, for I believe in early marriage and plenty of children who will also be my grandchildren. I long to be a wholesale grandmother. One's own children are a joy but also a responsibility. Has one done the best that could be done by them? This question haunts any intelligent parent. But of grandparents nothing is required except much love and secret spoiling, which if it turns out badly, will all be blamed on the parents.

I inherit my anticipation of grandparenthood from my years in China. Grandparents there had such a good time! They opened their arms and made shelter when parents were angry and scolding. They produced tidbits of forbidden sweets. They spent hours taking their grandchildren to see street shows and wasted vast numbers of pennies in hiring jugglers and monkeys to come and perform through long afternoons in the courtyards. Children told their grandparents all their secrets, the things they could not tell their parents, who felt responsible for them. When my time comes, I shall be a reckless and irresponsible grandmother.

In still another way I envy the Chinese grandmothers. Chinese families have the pleasure of helping to choose the people their children marry. Of course, modern young China has rebelled against this to some extent, but it remains true that over the most of China the family still has a great deal to say about sons' wives and daughters' husbands. What an exciting time it is, what discussions take place in the family council, what weighing and matching of personalities! The beloved child, grown to the need of a mate, is analyzed as carefully as any Western psychologist could do it, but for love and not for money. Childhood is retraced and inclinations considered. Against the known of the child, the parents match the unknown youth, male or female, who will suit the child as well as the family.

The Chinese are wise enough to know that any individual is inescapably part of the family and that he will be happier in love if his mate also pleases his family. Emotional security will be assured and complete only if there is family acceptance, too. So horoscopes are compared, the stars under which the two young people were born are consulted, the hour, even to the very moment, of their births, even of their conception in the wombs of their mothers, the weather at the time of birth, their temperaments, their experience, their likes and dislikes, their looks and manners. When the best possible match between male and female is found and decided upon, then what solemnity of betrothal there is, what gifts are exchanged, what courtesies and compliments, what pride and self-respect on both sides!

In the old days, the young were not consulted in all this matchmaking, but nowadays in up-to-date families, at least, the young pair are approached and questions are put as to tastes, likes, and repulsions. Chinese parents have learned something, too, and they know now that it is well if between the young pair there is that intangible attraction—perhaps more physical than spiritual at first—which is an essential for enduring marriage and yet which alone is not enough to insure it.

Sometimes, of course, the young being what they are anywhere, parents find that a choice has already been made. Then the whole matter is gone at again, backward. The choice is still examined by all the old standards. If the parents reject what the child chooses, there comes a battle of wills, fought with courtesy and kindness, with tears and stubbornness, even with threatened suicide by the young, which probably brings surrender on the part of softhearted elders. Chinese elders are usually tender-hearted. However it is done, marriage is a matter for family concern and participation. For, the sensible Chinese reasons, when a young person marries he does so not only for himself. He brings someone into the family. The family has the right to object if the new member is objectionable. A son's wife is also a daughter-in-law, also a niece and sister-in-law, an aunt, perhaps, and certainly a cousin.

I confess I envy my Chinese friends. Here in America it seems that my sons' wives and my daughters' husbands are none of my business. I am to wait in silence until one day a person whom I have perhaps never seen appears at the door of our family house. Who is this person? Perhaps my son-in-law, perhaps the wife of my son! What frightful possibilities! Suppose he—she—is someone who can never fit into our family? What if I know that he is the wrong man for my daughter, she the impossible wife for my son? Somewhere even now these new relatives are growing up, are arriving at like maturity with my children, and the day will inevitably come when we must meet face to face. Of course, it is equally possible, perhaps even more than probable, that I shall like them. I can think of scores of young people whom I do like very much, and yet I know that this one, for example, or that one, to point out another, would be a wrong choice for my son or my daughter. Catholic though I am in this matter of liking almost everybody for something or other and never expecting to like anyone for everything, I myself could conceivably like a young man who might nevertheless be entirely the wrong man for a given daughter; and I might have a deep attachment to a young woman who nevertheless would make a very wrong wife for a given son. I am a little on the easy side, I am told. I do not think that, alone, I have the wisdom even to advise.

For that reason, I wish that I had the Chinese family system to lean upon in this matter of happy marriages for the children. If all the relatives could come together and give their judgment upon the proposed new relative, it would be a comforting thing. It would guide me as a mother-in-law. It would also serve as a check upon a rash son or daughter who might be taken by a pretty face or handsome looks. I would be a poor check, for I like pretty faces and handsome looks, too.

Lin Yutang, surveying the American scene, said one day that the most important decision in the life of Americans is made at the time when the judgment is most incompetent, namely, when people are in love.

Love, of course, is as inevitable to the young as chicken pox. The only question is when the children are to have it. Chinese parents, for many centuries, have set the time as physiological. Romance comes upon the flood of adolescence. The Chinese family watched the flood and took it at high tide. They chose and presented the young girl to the youth at the moment when his mind was obsessed simply with the wonder of the female. Thus, too, the daughter was bestowed at the precise moment when she began to dream of being a wife. The close-knit Chinese family perceived when the young broke from the old.

I, too, perceive but I am helpless. In our country, it is not proper for parents to notice the fact that their children ought to marry, even though it is obvious. It is not polite to notice the pursuit of the sexes, each for the other, even though it takes place and indeed is entirely right and proper. It is accepted that parents must keep out of the marriage game beyond a mild exposure of the young to each other in social affairs. Even too many of these set the teeth of the young on edge. But custom alone does not check my impulse to be helpful to my children in this most important decision of their lives—one very important to their family, too. The children themselves forbid any expression of anxiety or of eagerness on my part. Wistful hopes for grandchildren are sternly ignored. Preferences expressed for this or that young person as a possible mate are met with scorn. Yes, I understand humbly that the people my children marry are none of my business.

Yet they *are*. Alone in my heart I know the Chinese are right. At least they are partly right. I observe that there are fewer unhappy marriages under their system than under ours. Wisdom is a necessary ingredient in any marriage. If two people have it, any marriage can be a success. If one of the two has it, there is a sporting chance for success. If neither has it, the marriage cannot last, and the test of any marriage is whether it lasts. Chinese marriages do last as long as the families had a part in making them. Whether they are all happy depends on the alternative, if the marriage is broken. Nobody yet has devised a cure for the unhappy marriage except a happy one, and I firmly believe that the chances for a happy marriage are better if the family council sits. More heads are wiser than one.

We Americans are beginning to understand this now, too. The reckless individualism of the past is finding modification in the marriage courts, the sex instruction classes, and the divorce-menders. Unfortunately, too much of this is remedial rather than preventive and takes place after the marriage begins to break up instead of before the ceremony, as in the Chinese family. The per-

centage of loss, therefore, must still run high. The time to
make ready for a successful marriage is before the
wedding. Moreover, it is more suitable, or so I think, for
such matters to be the concern of the family than of the
total stranger.

When I say family, I mean the large family, in all its
generations and ramifications. The lack of emotional
security of our American young people is due, I believe,
to their isolation from the large family unit. No two
people—no mere father and mother—as I have often said,
are enough to provide emotional security for a child. He
needs to feel himself one in a world of kinfolk, persons of
variety in age and sex and temperament, and yet allied to
himself by an indissoluble bond which he cannot break if
he would, for nature has welded him into it before he was
born. Our dangerously extreme individualism, inherited
from forebears who were rebels and left their homes to
roam in the solitary wilderness of a new country, has led
to a rejection of the family by every individual, in greater
or less degree. Children do not want their parents to live
with them when they set up for themselves, and parents
do not want to live with their children. They reject each
other mutually.

Yet in doing so they violate nature, and when nature is
violated the result is emotional insecurity. No creature is
entirely happy when he is entirely independent of those to
whom he belongs. His rejection of his family, moreover,
makes him the more sensitive to rejection by his own
children in time. Cutting himself off from the generation
before him, he clings to the one he has produced, seeking

unconscious comfort, and so is the more wounded when he is pushed away. Emotional balance and wholeness of spirit come only when young and old live together. The sex relationship of male and female is not enough, even for one generation. They need the connection to the past and to the future. Old people need grandchildren, and children need old people. Human life must stretch both ways before the eyes of any one generation, so that continuity is an everyday experience, and love is long and deep—the love of a large family and many persons, rather than love between two alone with a few children. For emotional health, we must return to the large family system.

But this will not be in my time. I shall have to adapt myself to things as they are. On any day I still have to face a youth who proposes to be not only my daughter's husband, let us say, but also my son-in-law. What if he is the wrong man? What can American parents do if their daughter, alone and unsupported by the family, wants to marry the wrong man? How does one even recognize the wrong man? Marriages here happen so quickly.

The first time we saw one young man he was already engaged to be our son-in-law. We had to take him, sight unseen. What if it happens again, as it might any day, and what if this time he really is that wrong man? Wrong for whom? Not for parents, certainly, for parents do not matter here—not in marriages. Wrong, I mean, for my daughter, wrong for her temperament, for her age, for her physical being. I am blessed with a variety of daughters. A brilliant, mercurial son-in-law would be all wrong for one of them. He must be protected, as well as she. Nor must he be one who craves maternal affection, for she is the cool career girl, levelheaded and, I confess it, a little selfish. Yet, should my small firebrand have such a husband, either? Left alone by either, would they not quarrel away this love?

And what of the shy daughter? How will she ever find a husband at all in this country where the whole burden of marriage is put upon the girl? My sons will have their choice according to their fitness, for any man can marry. But will some good and suitable man have the wisdom to find his loving and faithful wife in a quiet girl to whom God has given a rich heart but not a pretty face? Yet perhaps even the wrong man is better than none. Life is incomplete without marriage, and the fullness of life is what I want for my children, as for myself.

The wrong man is therefore entirely relative. My shy child might find her deepest joy in marrying a drunkard or a wastrel and trying to make a man of him. I would lock my skepticism in myself in that case and keep all doors open. Since marriage is an individual act in our civilization, theoretically there is no such person as the wrong man. Any man my daughter chooses is the right man. I can do nothing about it. In the old days when we had tradition rather than freedom, we parents could allow only young men we approved to frequent our houses. Now we do not always know even the last names of such young men.

I, for example, remember Bill, Vic, Jack, Ted—what? Their surnames, their homes, their families I cannot remember. In my old-fashioned way, I inquired of all these matters, important, it seemed, only to me, but never seen in the flesh, they have not stayed with me. I presume these young men were born of real parents, live, at least briefly, in houses somewhere, and come of a certain ancestry. But for me none of these things are so. For me they have simply appeared, spectrally alone, and may disappear in the same way. I grow alarmed at the possibility of a permanent relationship with some one of these and meditate on the possibility of slipping off alone with an address scribbled upon a bit of paper to discover the family with which I may have to share my grandchildren. My daughter may not be so particular, but I want my grandchildren to inherit equally well on both sides. I want to look the other family over, and in fairness to them, to disclose to them our worst as well as our best. We owe it to each other, for the sake of the unborn.

Suppose, after this fantastic conference, which would certainly enrage the two most concerned if they knew of it, we decided that their son was the wrong man for our daughter, which would make her equally the wrong girl for him. What could we do? In the old days the girl was whisked off to Europe while the boy stayed at home, or the young man took the grand tour while the girl married someone else before he came back. Our young people would not stand for this now, of course. The elders could never accomplish it. No, the two families can do nothing when the wrong mate is chosen except watch their young people leap over the precipice of marriage.

Actually, in such an individualistic society as ours now

is—destructively individualistic in some of its aspects—the only security against an unfortunate marriage lies in long and early education. Eugenics and psychology, the inexorable principles of science, must take the place of family wisdom. Marriage is the most important part of any individual's life. It is far more than an event. It is the maturity toward which life shapes from the moment of birth.

The choice of a mate, if it is to be left to the individual, should be the subject of years of careful preparation. Yet in most American families it is scarcely mentioned, I discover, except as a subject for jokes and teasing. Out of this environment, our young people approach in haphazard ignorance the most profound and important choice of their entire lives, a choice that means happiness or sorrow. The wonder is not that there are so many unhappy marriages and so many divorces, but that there are so few in proportion to what could only be expected, given what is. It is mere luck when it is not the wrong man.

All this is very old-fashioned musing on my part. And yet, if one is old-fashioned enough, one is new-fashioned. Taking out of its silver wrapping paper my grandmother's wedding gown of ivory satin and rose point lace, I see that it will do very well for my small and most turbulent daughter if she will consent to have her waist pinched in a bit for an hour or so while the guests congratulate her. The styles have come around again. Maybe they will come around again in families, too. I hope so.

I'd like Uncle John's estimate of young Fred, for example, who is beginning to look suspiciously like a son-in-law. Will he be able to deal with our daughter's tempers? I am ashamed of them and I would like to apologize to him for them. If I had had a big family close to help me teach her control, it would have been easier. Fred looks too gentle. I wouldn't want a man with a whip, but I'd like a man with a loud laugh. A mother's laughter wounds and does not heal; a lover's laughter is different. I know a woman who had childish tempers until long after middle age when, marrying her third husband, she was cured abruptly because he found her so ridiculous in a temper that he laughed uncontrollably. The other two husbands had been gentle ones. I like gentle people and I would enjoy Fred as a son-in-law, but I can see that he is really the wrong man.

Families cannot choose just for themselves, either. There must be justice in love, too. If this develops in spite of me, I may be reduced to the humiliation of warning the son-in-law I would like to have by reading him a lesson from *The Taming of the Shrew*. Yet I must not oppose the choice openly, lest to my daughter it should appear that I am going beyond my privilege as a parent. I can only try to tell her that she will not be happy with a man she can bully and possess. Even if she thinks she would enjoy it, she must marry her equal, a man who can win at least half the time. Otherwise he will be the wrong man for her. She will tell me to mind my own business—not rudely, for she has been well brought up, but in terms which I, who watched every expression on her baby face, can well understand. To which I shall reply that this *is* my business, for she is choosing my son-in-law and the father of my grandchildren. I may even tell her I consider it my duty to tell Fred about last week when she lost her temper again because . . . I forget why, now. I always forget as quickly as I can.

But of course I know I shall not tell Fred anything. The human race marks time, century after century, because the generations learn nothing from each other if they are given the freedom to refuse to learn. History really is bunk, as Henry Ford once said, but not because lessons are not there to be learned. The pages are rich with instruction but only for those who seek it. Perhaps the young never seek it. How much restiveness was hidden behind the submissive faces of the young Chinese I used to know, how much rebellion in the hearts of young brides and grooms? Well, if it was all there, they dealt with it in the secret places of their own souls. They learned what used to be called sublimation while they fulfilled the duties and reared the children of the new generation. And quite often, far more often than one would expect, they fell in love after marriage, a blessed, growing love crowned by the surrounding approval of family and tradition, a pleasant sight for parents to behold.

Yes, I still believe that families are important. Someday I may even get up the courage to tell my children so. But being American, would they understand?

8

What Shall I Tell My Daughter?

S HE is to be married. I see that at once as she comes to my door. I am as usual at my desk, but this room, dedicated to my work and my art, is always open to my child. She is, of course, no longer a child. She is twenty years old, and I have known for the last two years that some morning she would stand at my door, looking at me shyly with that peculiar radiance which love and only love gives to a woman. She can never achieve it alone, however sacred the cause to which she dedicates herself. It is only when she knows the man whom she loves loves her that her eyes glow with the mysterious light, her skin takes on translucence, her cheeks flush, her lips part in half-smiling joy at once innocent and profound.

"Come in, my darling," I say.

"Are you busy?" she inquires, not so much in concern for my work as in hesitation. How can she convey to me the extraordinary news? Will I understand that a young man who was only recently a little boy with grubby hands and mischievous face, a gangling youth whose hair was unbrushed and too long, a callow young man who went off to college. . . .

"I have something to tell you," she informs me.

She comes in, sits down in the worn armchair and spreads her pink skirts. She looks very pretty this morning, quite apart from love. Her dark hair is shining with health and good grooming, her skin is tanned by the summer sun, and her lips are red with natural health.

"You look very nice today—even nicer than usual," I say by way of encouragement.

She does not appear to hear my remark. Ah well, she is accustomed to being told that she is beautiful. Her violet eyes, set in long, black lashes under fine, dark brows, are grave with purpose.

"Mother?"

"Yes, my child?"

"I suppose you have noticed that he and I—"

I cannot resist a teasing impulse. "He? Darling, which 'he' do you mean?"

Young men surround her and there are at least four whom I imagine as quite possible in varying ways—four, that is, whom I would find acceptable as. . . .

"Mother!" she exclaims in horror. "As if it could be anyone but Peter!"

Peter? But I have not thought of Peter. I thought of course it would be—and why Peter? She has only known him for six months. He is seven years older than she is. That is to say, twenty-seven is much older than twenty. At twenty-seven a man has already been in love several times, in all probability, and she has never been in love before—not like this!

"Peter?" I cannot hide my surprise.

"But you said you liked him!" Her eyes, very blue and accusing, open wide and fill with unexpected tears.

I leave my seat at once and run to her side.

"Darling, of course I like him. I just don't think you know him well enough for—"

"I knew the moment I saw him. And he knew. He proposed to me within the week."

"You didn't—"

"Oh no, I didn't accept him at once. I remembered what you said about that—you said you married too quickly the first time and that was why there had to be a second time, when you were really in love. I waited for six months to pass."

"Six months?" I repeat stupidly. I sit down on the big hassock at her feet.

She is impatient with me. "You said—don't you remember?—a girl should know a man for six months at least. Well, it was six months last night, at quarter past eight, and he stood beside me under the sycamore tree at the end of the lane, his watch in his hand until the minute came up—"

We both laugh. She leans forward to give me a quick embrace and releases me as quickly.

"Of course," she goes on, smoothing her skirt, "they were unnecessary, those six months."

"I am not so sure," I retort. "You may be glad for them later."

She pays no heed to this. It is obvious that she hears nothing I say. She pushes back her dark hair.

"We don't want a long engagement," she announces.

"Which is to tell me that you want to be married as soon as possible," I retort.

"Next month, on the fifteenth, at four o'clock. It's a special date, a special hour."

I do not allow myself to ask questions. Her memories are already sacred to herself and to him. She is not looking at me. She is looking at her hands, folded on her lap. One hand is over the other.

"Let me see your ring," I say.

She holds up her left hand. A single diamond, not too large, for she is petite, this child of mine, but a fine, clear diamond, not too small either, and beautifully set, shines on her third finger.

"He had it all ready for me," she tells me softly.

"He was sure of you, then?"

"Of course," she says with calm.

I marvel at the honesty of my child. In this she is a true daughter of her times. The old fencing between man and woman, the ancient coquetries, are cast aside, it seems. She is not in the least ashamed of her readiness to love this man Peter.

We sit in silence for a moment, I still holding her left hand as I consider Peter. Will he be tender with her? Will he understand her need for solitude? Will he love her little willful ways? There is so much of the child in her still and always must be, I think. She has a native innocence, the sense of reality which children have—and very great people also.

She draws her hand away gently and covers it again with her right hand, as something too dear, too personal, too close, even for me to see or to hold.

The strange pause continues between us. She breaks it, and, to my surprise, with tears again in her eyes.

"Oh, Mother—" her voice chokes in a half sob.

"What is it, my darling? Why do you cry?"

"I don't know! Perhaps I'm afraid . . . a little—"

"Afraid? Not of him?"

"Of . . . of love . . . of not being able to make him happy. He is so intelligent . . . much more than I am. You know that. He is clever and . . . and educated . . . and . . . and. . . ."

This is true. Peter is an intellectual, a young scientist, an artist in his area. I know the type. My child is also well educated, but not in the same field. A mathematical equation means nothing to her while to Peter it is his language.

"Oh, Mother!" she wails. Her head is suddenly on my shoulder. I feel her soft hair on my cheek. "If he ever stops loving me . . . I'll die!"

I smooth back the hair and feel the flushed cheek. "Now, now," I say in my most practical voice, "how do you think he would feel if you stopped loving him? He'd want to die, too—perhaps."

I add the "perhaps" for caution and she comprehends.

She lifts her head and wipes the tears away with her small handkerchief, pulled from her belt.

"No, he wouldn't," she says flatly. "Men don't. They have so many things to think about. That's what I'm afraid of. He could stop loving me without realizing it . . . sort of . . . you know, the way men do."

"Women do, too, sometimes," I put in.

She shakes her head at this. Impossible, the violet eyes declare, incredible that she should ever stop loving Peter!

"Oh yes," I maintain. "If one stops loving, the other does, too. It's mutual, this falling in love—and out again."

"Oh no!" she cries with passion. "I don't want to stop loving him. What shall I do? I don't know about love . . . not really, not enough!"

I cannot answer her at once. What shall I tell my daughter about love? It takes thinking. There is so much to tell. I cannot overwhelm her with my own experience, I, who know the many ways in which a man can be loved—yes, and be taught to love—for I am not sure that men know by instinct, as women do, what love is. They are confused and complicated by the powerful drive of physical sex, so much more simple and single than the woman's sexual drive. If she is not wary and wise and sensitive and, above all, if she does not love him enough, the relationship degenerates. The marriage becomes the humdrum of every day. The magic is gone.

Yet it is not true that this is inevitable—too usual, perhaps, but not inevitable. And it is the woman's—what is the right word?—not task, not duty, a little of these, but joy is the essence. It is the woman's joy to keep love at the level of delight and companionship and, yes, and of romance. It is a word misused and made contemptible by cheap people in cheap ways, but a word of rich emotion in spite of that.

"Leave me a little while, darling," I tell my child. "Go and find Peter. I'm sure he's waiting for you. When you are alone again, I'll be ready for you. I must sort things out in my own mind—what's important and what isn't."

She rises with such alacrity that I know Peter is waiting outside the door. I am right.

"Come in, Peter," she cries. "I've told her."

The door opens. I like what I see. He stands there, tall and slim and slightly embarrassed. He has brushed his fair hair with unusual care and he has forgotten his glasses. I see his dark eyes clearly. They are tender and humorous.

"Good morning," he says and stops. How does one go on from there? He makes a brave effort. "I hope you are not shocked."

"Shocked?" I repeat the word and let it hang for an instant.

He tries to be nonchalant. He sits down. "Dare I hope you are pleased?"

"You may hope," I reply cruelly. "I shall find out after the years pass. This child is my treasure."

He puts aside all pretense. "I know," he says in a low voice. "And I am too old for her perhaps. Too much of an intellectual and all that? But she is my treasure, too. I cannot live without her. I have not thought of a woman since I first saw her walking down the street one day last spring. She passed me and I looked back at her and she looked back at me. It began in that moment. It will go on forever."

He is so earnest that I want to believe him.

"I hope so," I tell him. "And of course I am pleased that she is happy. Now leave me, my children. I have work to do."

They leave me, hand in hand and forgetting to close the door. I close it, but I do not return to my desk. I sit down in the worn armchair. I lean back and close my eyes. My life comes flooding in upon the tides of memory. I have been in love—yes, more than once. I have loved men in different ways, for different reasons. I still love. One never grows too old. That is a discovery. Man or woman, we never grow too old for love. I say it is a discovery, for when young I supposed that love belonged only to youth. And yet, when I was halfway through my life, I fell in love again and it seemed to me that it was for the first time. Years passed, happy years, and when they were ended and I was left alone, I said to myself that now love was over. I had loved my heart out and I could not love again. Then I made the discovery. The heart does not die. It maintains its habits of love. Not the same, it is true, for the ways of the heart are manifold and of infinite variety.

Shall I tell my child this truth? No! She is too young to know. Let her believe what she must believe now—that this is her one and only love. There must be no shadow of the future. It will fall upon her at the destined hour, and life itself will have prepared her for change—life or death. I will speak to her of something more important than love. I will speak to her of herself.

I will say to her something like this:

"The question is not whether you ever stop loving him or he ever stops loving you. The question is, do you know who you are? Well, I will tell you. You are a woman. In many ways you are a fortunate woman. You have beauty, you have intelligence. But these are perquisites and not necessities. They are gifts for which you should be thankful, and which you should use to the utmost. But if you had not these gifts, you would still be a woman and you would still have the necessity to know what it means to be a woman.

"You ask what this means? It means that you are a creation entirely different from man. True, nature does not discriminate between male and female in the distribution of her gifts. A daughter may inherit the brains, and not the son. She may have much while he may have little. Yet the fact that you have intelligence does not mean that it is the same intelligence the man has. Your intelligence is expressed through your woman material, and it is not the same as the man material. It is as though clear spring water were poured into a rose-red glass bowl and appeared rose red. If the same spring water were poured into a blue-glass bowl it would appear blue. Essentially it is the same but the container changes the hue. You will have the same impulses that Peter has, certainly the same need for love, but it will be expressed differently.

"He will express his love with ardor and frequency through physical sex, for example. To him it is the way he can best express his love. Warm words, kisses, embraces so precious to you, so needed, are needed by him, too, but as introduction to the final demand of his body. Ah yes, you will agree to this finale, you will respond, at times welcome it and at times even invite it, but it will be the last step, not always essential. For him it is first and all-important.

You are to remember, then, that you are woman. Your

love permeates your whole being. You are fortunate in the many ways you have of expressing love. To arrange his house, to plan his meals, to care for his comfort, to serve him—yes, I insist upon the word, for such service is sacred to love, even in the simplest and most menial ways. Menial? Nothing is menial where there is love.

"I tell you frankly that you must teach him the many ways of expressing love. The whole joy of sex is not in a single act. It is a prevailing atmosphere, a pervading life between man and woman, uniting in love two separate and different beings. He is a direct and sometimes blundering creature, this man. If he does not please you, laugh at him a little, but tenderly, and lead him along pleasant paths to the full understanding of your woman nature. Do not expect him to learn without being taught. If you do not teach him, some other woman may—or may already have done so. Above all, do not blame him for ignorance about you. You see why you must not be ignorant about yourself. If you do not understand yourself as a woman, how can you teach him?

"And let him teach you about himself. Do not pretend to know everything. You are ignorant about him because you are not a man, just as he is ignorant about you because he is not a woman. Teach one another and rejoice in being so taught. The more each knows of the other, the happier both will be. And you will never know everything, either of you, for in this mutual teaching—from the smallest detail, as for example how he likes his coffee, to the deepest and most profound matter of private love—you will discover that you are both growing and develop-

ing and reaching new levels of emotion and intelligence.
There is nothing so fertilizing to the growth of the individual man and woman as the love between them, a growing, living love, which is to say, true, love. He will never
stop loving you if he finds something always new in you,
and through you in himself. Nor will you ever stop loving
him. Love dies only when growth stops.

What was it that a wise old Chinese said five hundred
years before our Christian era? A disciple asked him
whether a certain way was the right way, and Lao-tze
replied: "It is a way, but not the eternal way."

You may test the truth of your love by your own growth
as a woman and his as a man. If you are both growing in
happiness, improving in mind and body, then your way of
loving is the eternal way.

Yet do not worry yourself or even inquire of yourself as
to whether you are growing. You will know that you are
growing, for love will keep you informed. You will be
happy—yes, even though there may be occasional disagreement. I will not use the word quarrel, for only
children quarrel, without regard to facts or truth. Never
descend to such trifling behavior with him. It is not
important to know *who* is right. It is only important to
know *what* is right. And you will discover that truth
together and only together. A one-sided conclusion, declared by one against the other, will be only a half truth
and worth nothing. The one who insists and prevails by
insistence takes the first step toward the death of love. Do
not compete with him, for competition is impossible between you. Neither can lose and neither wins. I deny the

battle of the sexes. If we do battle, then the battle is already lost and for both. Victory is only to be achieved in unity—victory over life and, yes, over death.

"Accept your womanhood, my daughter, and rejoice in it. It is your glory that you are a woman, for this is why he loves you, he whom you love. Be gentle, be wise, as a woman is gentle and wise. Be ardent and love with a woman's ardor. Through your love, teach him what it means to be a man, a noble man, a strong man. Believe in him, for only through your belief can he believe in himself. In our secret hearts, man and woman, we long above all else to know that the other, the one we love, knows what we are and believes in what we can be. Is this not romance? Yes, and the highest romance, investing the smallest detail of life with the color of joy.

"You observe, my darling child, that I say nothing of the duties of housewifery or motherhood or care of your person or even of the preservation of your beauty and charm. All such duties are easy enough to perform if you have this knowledge of yourself as woman. For if you know yourself as woman, you will comprehend your own need of him, your primary and profound need. Without him, you are only half a woman, as without you he is less than a man. Stay together, you two—never let him go, and never leave him, once your love is established and alive. Stay together, cling hand in hand, walk step in step, sleep close, so that you know forever that you are not alone!"

9

Shall I Marry the Father of My Child?

THE MORNING'S MAIL is piled on my desk. On top is a small cream-white envelope, my name written upon it in a clear, firm hand. The postmark is the City of New York. Millions of people in New York, and why should I wonder about this letter? Nevertheless I open it.

The contents are not unusual. A young woman, a stranger, is in trouble. I know at once what the trouble is. She is to have a child—my eyes rove quickly down the page. Yes, it is a child. May she come and see me and ask my advice?

I examine the letter. The young woman is articulate and well educated. She is probably one of the many young women who live alone and independent in the vast city, finding love as they can, avoiding it and yet seeking it. The address is good enough to mean that she makes a fair salary. She need not marry for money. She can support herself, and the child can be placed for adoption or put in a boarding home. None of this is unusual. It is, in fact, a very old story. Why should I take the time to see her? It is not my responsibility to decide so personal a matter. I decide not to see her. I shall write a letter and tell her that many young women have her problem, an increasing number in these changing times. I am sorry that I have not time to give to all and therefore must not give to one who—

Before I go further, the telephone rings. A soft voice announces a stranger, a woman, and young, as I can tell by the timbre of the voice.

"Have you my letter?" she inquires, after greetings.

"I have, but only today and I was about to—"

"Don't say you can't see me!" she exclaims. "I know I have no right to ask you for precious time, but I do ask it."

Something moves me. Pleading I can resist but there is more than pleading here. There is desperation.

"Where are you?" I inquire.

"Very near you. I mailed my letter yesterday and followed it on the train. I can be with you in ten minutes."

I cast a look of consternation at the work on my desk. Then I yield. There is something I like about the voice.

"Very well. Then come."

It takes me ten minutes of floor pacing to collect my thoughts on the subject of children born out of wedlock. I have known many such children. Years ago, with the help of friends, I founded an adoption agency known as Welcome House. Through our offices, hundreds of children have passed from hospitals and orphanages to loving, happy adoptive families. I know all too well the woman with the child but with no husband to be its father. I have seen such women, young and not so young. I have seen them ignorant and simpleminded, but I have also seen them as daughters in some of our best families. Which would this one be?

She is announced. "A young woman to see you, madam."

I can tell by the tone of the gardener's voice that he does not approve this young woman. He does not approve any young woman who appears at my door in a state of distress, especially if she is pretty. And this one I can see is very pretty. She is standing outside the door, waiting and anxious. I go to meet her.

"Come in, please!"

The hand I take in mine is feverishly warm. She comes in, a tall, graceful girl, dark hair, dark eyes set in a sensitive, intelligent face. She wears a well-cut brown suit with a narrow fur collar.

"Sit down, please," I tell her.

She sits down in the green armchair beside the fire. She says not one word but watches me, her large eyes mournful and perhaps frightened. I make talk as I put a log on the fire.

"It is cold today—I think we shall have snow before night. Autumn comes so quickly—only a few short weeks between summer and winter."

She still says nothing. She waits until I am seated on the other side of the hearth. She continues to look at me.

I see her lips quiver and I take the lead firmly. "Now, my dear, please be at ease. Other young women like you have sat in that chair and looked at me as you are doing now. I quite understand how you feel. So tell me what is in your heart."

It is not so easy. A simple girl, one not so well brought up could begin more easily. But she has been trained to reserve. I try to help her.

"You have come to ask that your baby be adopted?"

"I—I don't know yet."

"You have other plans?"

"No. That is—I don't know what to plan. Everything depends. . . ."

She pauses but we have made a start. Her face, ashen pale, takes on a faint flush.

"Depends on your parents?"

"Oh no. They know nothing about my . . . situation."

"You do not wish them to know?"

"I have another question to answer first. As I said . . . everything depends on. . . ."

Beyond this she is unable to proceed. I know the point.

"You are to be married first, perhaps?"

I know she is not. If she were to be married, she would not be here in this room now. Her problem would be solved.

"I don't know," she said finally.

The time has come now for gentle pressure.

"The Chinese," I begin, "have a wonderful phrase for people who are anxious. '*Fang hsin*,' they would say to you. That means release your heart. Free your heart, my dear. In this room you are safe. Suppose you begin at the beginning. Is the man married? It is the most important fact at this moment."

"No, he is not."

"Then he is free to marry you?"

"Yes . . . if he wants to . . . or and if I want him to."

"You are in love with him?"

"I . . . think so."

"You think so? You don't know?"

She hesitates. "When I am with him, I am in love with him."

I put the one question, the important one, which I have held back until now. "Does he know about the baby?"

"No."

The answer is quiet. I draw a breath of relief. I smile at her with loving understanding. I know now why she has come to me. She comes with an old, old question. If she were less sensitive, less intelligent, she would not be here. She would answer it for herself impulsively by demanding that the man marry her at once.

I speak for her now. "You have come to ask me whether you should tell him about the child."

She lifts her head, eyes full of wonder. "How did you know?"

I shake my head, still smiling. "I know. You are not the first one. Tell me about this man."

The flush on her beautiful face deepens. "He is older than I am. Ten years."

"Still young," I reply. "You are what? Twenty? Twenty-two?"

"Twenty-four. I finished college two years ago. I got a job in New York because I wanted to do something. My family is the old-fashioned sort. They live in Boston. My mother . . . well, she would simply never understand what has happened or how it could happen. She didn't want me to leave home. And my father . . . well, he wouldn't understand either. He would only lose his temper—"

I break in. "What has happened cannot be changed. The question is, what of the future?"

She lifts her head, she looks me straight in the eyes. "What do you tell the others?"

I answer her as directly. "I tell them that I cannot make their decision. I can only tell them what they must face, however they decide. If you decide not to tell this man that you are to have a child by him, then you must, of course, cease to see him. You will have to think of your own way to do this. You must simply disappear from his life. What, then, will be your situation? It depends upon whether you decide to give your child up for adoption. If you decide to do so, then you may return to your life in New York, but I hope never again to this relationship with him. You cannot escape without pain, in any case.

"You may think you wish to give up your child but in your heart you will never give him up. You will think of him again and again. Yes, you have the legal right to see him before you make up your mind but if you do, it will only be the harder to give him up. His little face, so innocent, will remain with you as long as you live. You will see him in other children as he grows, a little boy, a big boy, a young man, a man, your son wherever he is. You will not know where he is. Once you have yielded him, by law you have no further right over him. He belongs to other people, his mother someone else. But he will have a father. With this you may comfort yourself. He will have a father as well as a mother. And they will love him or they would not have taken him for their own. We have good adoption laws here in the United States. It requires parents to treat the adopted child exactly as though he, or she, were born to them, including inheritance."

Her eyes were swimming with tears. "What if I keep him?"

"If you keep him," I say gently, "then a heavy burden falls upon him. Other children will ask where his father is. You will be compelled to lie to him. 'Your father is dead,' you will say. But truth is disconcerting. It has a way of coming out by its own power at its own time. One never knows. The child may look like the man. The man may suspect. Or, if you never see the man again, the truth will force its own way out of you, somehow. Your friends will know you are not married. You will be compelled to change your whole world, leave your family and start again somewhere as a young widow. And if you fall in love one day and marry a good man, what will you say to him? Can you keep this lie alive forever? You cannot."

"Oh, it is too cruel," she sobs.

"Very cruel, I agree. I can only say that we live in

changing times. Each year in our country some 250,000
children are born out of wedlock. They are called illegitimate, but it is the man and the woman who are the
lawbreakers. There are no laws to protect the child born
to two persons who are not husband and wife. He is
helpless, born into a country, an age, which offer him no
protection. The child, in fact, has no legal right to be born
for he has neither home nor family. He is a displaced
person in the land of his birth.

"It is sad that the freedom between the sexes here in
our country leads men and women into intimacies which
cannot prevent the birth of children. Our laws have not
changed as our habits and mores have changed. The laws
are still strict and they do not recognize that standards
have changed. Most women, if we are to believe recent
statistics, are not virgins when they marry. The double
standard for men and women is no longer in existence
except in name. Because the law does not acknowledge
this, the burden falls heavily upon the woman and the
child and not upon the man."

She says something so muffled by weeping that I cannot
understand her and she has to repeat. "I say I have
already decided to give my child for adoption if I don't
tell the . . . the man, that is."

I see that it is time for me to be matter-of-fact, to be
practical, even to seem cold.

"Then that is one decision made," I say briskly. "Now
we can proceed to the next. Shall you tell the man, you
ask? The question cannot be answered by yes or no.
There are preliminary questions. The first one is this: If

there were no child, would you still wish this man to be your husband? It is the most important question of all."

I wait for a longer moment. She wipes her eyes. She takes her compact out of her handbag and mends the damage of tears to her face—a good sign—and I wait.

"No," she says at last and almost calmly. "I have asked that question myself, already. No, I couldn't be happy with him. On the other hand . . ."

She pauses and I wait again and so long that I am conscious of precious time passing.

"On the other hand?" I suggest gently.

She gives a slight start, as though she had forgotten what we were talking about. "Oh . . . well, it would solve many problems, of course, if he married me. I wouldn't have to part with my baby. And as I said, in a way, I love this man. I don't respect him, perhaps . . . he's not bad . . . but . . . well, he's not what I'd dreamed of marrying, let's say. Charming, too charming . . . but no, definitely he wouldn't make a good husband, not for me. He's not my type."

"And you don't love him enough to be reckless?"

She shakes her head. "No. If I did I wouldn't be here, would I?"

I agree to this with a smile and in silence.

She goes on. "Still, for the sake of the child, perhaps—"

I break in swiftly. "For the sake of the child, do not marry the man. If he will not make you a good husband, he will not be a good father for the child. The lack you feel in him as a man cannot be changed merely because he becomes a father, and especially a father under such conditions. Moreover, the very fact that you marry him because you must and he knows he marries you under a sort of compulsion—"

She interrupts: "He is in love with me."

"There are many kinds of love," I reply, "and especially for a man. For a man, love is first of all physical. A man without thought of marriage urges a girl to give herself to him and he says, 'I love you.' It is true, he does love her at that instant with a sort of love, but it is not the eternal love, the love that reaches deep into the very being of man and woman and makes them one. Well, you may say I am being idealistic. Perhaps I am. But marriage should follow when the two at least believe that they have the eternal love. They may be wrong, but for the moment, the hour, they must believe. You are entertaining the thought of marriage without this conviction. You are saying to yourself that for the child's sake—and I say do nothing for the child's sake for unless you do it for your own sake, it will only bring sorrow to the child, too. In the disaster of your marriage he will be destroyed."

She listens, her great, dark eyes fastened upon my face. "Suppose I did love him in this eternal way, as you put it—"

"In that case, you would not be here," I retort. "You would have run to him at once to tell him that you have his child in you."

She is too honest not to acknowledge that this is true. "I suppose you are right," she says slowly. She looks away from me now.

"I know I am right," I tell her. "It is the only answer I

have to all your questions. I cannot, I repeat, make your decision. But I can say that if you marry this man for any other reason than that you cannot live without him, the child is better off without him, too."

A long moment of silence hangs between us. Then she gets up from her chair. She puts out her hand and I take it. We stand there hand in hand.

"Thank you," she says. "Thank you very much. I feel as though I had been walking in fog. I cannot say I have come out into sunlight, but at least the fog has cleared away. I see the path."

"I am glad," I tell her.

Our hands part. She draws on her gloves slowly, her head drooping, her face thoughtful and sad, her eyes downcast. Then she looks up bravely.

"I want my baby to have the very best father and . . . and mother. Will you help me to find them?"

"Yes," I say. "I will help you."

She tries to smile, she turns away and, at the door, pauses for the briefest wave of her gloved hand.

Now she is gone, I sit down again at my desk.

ON CHILDREN

10

Man, Woman and Child

THE ETERNAL TRIANGLE of life is not the two women and a man or the two men and a woman that novels and plays hold dear as the material of plot. The real triangle is made up of three equal sides, and they are man, woman and child. And the perfect equilibrium of these three as individuals, and the balance in their relation to each other, makes up the true stuff of human life. It is a triangle in which all human beings are involved in one of the three ways at least, and usually in more than one. It is rare that the triangle is perfectly equilateral. More often, one side is long and strong, and the others short and weak, and then the triangle is an inharmonious thing. Sometimes two lines of it are equal and the connecting third is dwarfed by them and it is still inharmonious. And yet the triangle of man, woman, and child ought to be equilateral, for only when it is so are these three complete as individuals and complete as a whole.

Bearing in mind, then, this triangle as the symbol of what should be the ideal relationship of the three basic creatures of human life, let us consider for a while what is to be discovered about the pattern they do form in that place which they make together, the home.

Our American homes are wholly unlike the traditional Chinese homes I knew in my childhood. The triangle of man, woman, and child is their symbol. Man and woman separate themselves from all others into a solitude of two, and when the child is born he joins this close little world and, in a sense mystic, rapturous, and sometimes tragic, the three become one. The union is either deep and close or it is intolerable and there is no escape from it. There was always escape in the Chinese home. If the man and woman were ill-mated, they could escape from each other into the larger family. They could, if they liked, see almost nothing of each other. The child, too, could escape his parents easily and without being aware of it. The individual was more easily an individual in that large family. He escaped the hold of deep emotional ties, as well as their satisfaction, perhaps. Certainly he escaped their almost inevitable overshadowing of his own personality. Nor did he lack affection.

In the close, small American family, the primary problem, it seems to me, is the one of maintaining the proper balance between individual life and development and the union necessary to the most successful family life and in relating the whole to the world beyond. For when the family is small—that is, mother, father and child—the responsibility upon the parents is greatly increased. The care of the child, physical, emotional and mental, depends entirely upon those two who have their own relation to each other to consider and at the same time their own individualities. The many personalities in the large Chinese family undoubtedly had their frictions, but it is debatable at least whether the relations between them were not, from the very number of persons involved, more superficial and therefore less oppressive than the profound tie between a man and a woman who, for love, choose each other and independently of all others make their life together. In the variety of the Chinese family, there was refuge from any one personality, but in the primary world of two, there is no refuge from each other. Deeper the joy, perhaps, but deeper, too, the wounds, and more inescapable.

Certainly the small American family does not, in its very structure, train the child naturally and unconsciously for the world outside. The adjustment from home to outside life is severe. The American home indeed forces the child into a peculiarly contradictory position. It provides a very deep and close emotional life and much and seclusive protection up to a certain age and then ejects the child into outside life with an abruptness that would horrify many an older culture, including the traditional Chinese.

The American home is not like the home in any other country. It is still a pioneer home, a relic of days when the adventurous man and woman left the settlement and pushed into the wilderness. The ability to be solitary, independent and resourceful and self-sufficient was necessary for the pioneer home, and these qualities inevitably developed. And since the pioneer became a symbol of American-

ism, his home became the ideal American home. To go out
for one's self, to build for one's own, became American virtues; and fine virtues they are and not to be lost.

But it is necessary to question whether or not the
pioneer home fits our no-longer-pioneer times. We have
come to the place that other older nations have reached,
of having to adjust our human beings and even their
ideals to their times. Thus we have to come to the point of
accepting the fact that the generations must help each
other more, the elder to help the younger by making
properly early marriage possible, and the younger by
helping to make old age secure. Either the home or the
state must do this. We are tending toward state care,
especially for the elderly, and we do not yet know the
effects that this will have upon the home and the individual. Certainly it seems only reasonable to believe that,
human nature being what it is, a person would be less
demoralized by family aid than by state aid. He sees the
sacrifice of others in the family but state funds are remote
and apparently inexhaustible, and persons soon learn to
take such help for granted. Perhaps it should be taken for
granted in the future state, but if it is, then the ideals of
individual independence must change if character is not
to deteriorate.

As I proceed it seems to me that perhaps the real problem of the American home today is entirely comprehended
in this lack of adjustment between its pioneer form and the
no-longer-pioneer times. For of the three, man and child
have proceeded with the times but woman has not, and today the home is peculiarly hers. Industrial development

has taken man out of the home. His workshop is no longer there but in a place not only physically remote but spiritually remote from woman. She used to know, and so to some extent share, what man did when he cleared land, cut down trees or worked at forge or harness or tavern. But now she does not share; she does not even know what man does. She remains in the pioneer age and is today a creature peculiarly alone.

Now even her child has been taken from her by the change of time. The child used to be her job, in addition to all her work of keeping the home, preparing food and clothing. She used to teach him how to read and write, and always supplemented, as far as she was able, the inadequate pioneer schools. But the schools are no longer pioneer, and the child has moved with the school. He leaves the home at the age of six or earlier, compulsorily, and from then on is returned to woman only for a few of the waking hours.

When women say, therefore, that their place today is in the home, it is a lonely place. The average American woman in the home of average income is far too much alone. It is, I think, a devastating loneliness. For she was once a part of her world, and if it was a world of wilderness, still, man and child were with her and together they made a comforting, companionable unit. But now she has not that companionship. She listens to as much as they will tell her, she reads as much as she is inclined, she potters about on the fringe of the world that really goes on without her, and comforts herself at least by having a good hot dinner ready at night. It is not enough. The feeling one has after coming to know American women is that they are starving at their sources. And the sources of woman are man and child, as she is a part of their sources.

Let me quote from a letter from an American woman, a college professor's wife. She says: "To those of us who have thought a good deal about woman's plight, it has become a truism that the work which made woman a productive force and gave her feeling of importance has been taken from the home. But the average woman does not realize this; she cannot understand why her house-wifely state is not socially satisfying, and, consequently, along with her restlessness goes a destructive sense of guilt."

I believe this woman is right. For the quality of American woman is high. She is natively intelligent, she has a higher education on the average than woman has in any other country. She has, unless she stifles it with tradition, a sensitive conscience. She wants to be of use and to use her powers. But having been left behind, she does not know what to do. She is not able to make even her home a part of the changing times. She struggles to keep it traditional, the place of shelter and refuge it once had to be in the wilderness instead of part of the world, as it now should be.

That early American home was the center of civilization, the only seat of learning, the one resource of the humanities, and to woman the man and child looked for spiritual comfort and counsel. But now civilization and learning and the humanities, as well as the livelihood, are found outside the home. And more serious to woman even than the removal of the need for her physical labor, is the fact that she is no longer the spiritual and moral influence she was once to man and child in the home. A woman cannot be a source of spiritual power to those two who live apart from her, in a vivid, changing world. Their problems are not hers. There is not time to tell her over again all that they have lived in the hours while they have been away from her. If woman is to recapture the lost companionship with man and child, she must once more forget herself, as she did in the old pioneer days, and follow them into the world.

I stress woman thus because I believe her situation is the main root of the problem in the American home today. Her restlessness and loneliness, whether she is aware of it or not, is an irritant in the home. In loneliness, she puts forth appeals, in one way or another, for companionship from these two. They are, according to their natures, either irked or oppressed by these appeals. And yet, she has been alone all day. Of course, no one except herself is to blame that she has been alone and lonely. But she does not see that, either. And yet, so good an intelligence has this woman, so fine an honesty and swift an energy, that I am convinced that if she can only be brought to see what her true situation has become, she will come out of it at any cost to herself.

The American woman has fallen into certain mistakes. She has, for instance, fallen into the mistake of accepting her separation from men. A young married woman said to me the other day: "We have come to take it for granted that we are married to perpetually tired men. The competition is so fearful these days that it takes all of our men's time just to make a living."

She looked so plump, so healthy, so little tired, that I could not forbear saying: "But why don't you work, too, so he isn't so tired and so that you can enjoy each other?"

She said, laughing, "Oh well, it seems as though everything was organized the way it is—it's hard to change things."

If this is the spirit of many American women, then of course they will simply drift into further segregation and into real uselessness and end, in some future age, in harems and zenanas, and our civilization will be degenerate and ended, and democracy dead. For no country is a true democracy whose women have not an equal share in life with men, and no country can hope to be a democracy whose women do not even want that share.

But I cannot believe that this is the spirit of many American women. The pioneer blood in them cannot be so dead. For the pioneer was willing to leave all he knew and go out and build the world he wanted. Change did not frighten him. There must, in our country, be women of spirit enough to want to grow with the nation and to stay beside man as he struggles to build. If there are not, then I say that the average woman in the home is the weakest link in American democracy, and by her weakness she drags at the man and hampers the child by her very love and devotion to them, if that love and devotion are not great enough, not intelligent enough, to comprehend the necessity of sharing their lives with them outside the home, as well as the few precious hours within it.

But who can help her to see this? Women must help her, exceptional, not-average women who, as individuals, have forged ahead for themselves. These women do not and have not given sufficient thought to the plight of the average woman who, because she has not their special gifts, has not had their peculiar means for progress with the times. I regard with alarm the distance between the comparatively few exceptional women in the United States and the average woman. It is not the proportion that is alarming but the distance between them. The exceptional woman is too often selfish and contemptuous in her attitude toward other women, too eager to prove that she herself is as competent and able as a man. But she should not forget that she is a woman and that only as all women progress will the nation benefit even by the exceptional woman.

Let us not forget that exceptional women had achieved very high place in Germany, and that even in the Reichstag itself there were once forty women members. Yet, with Nazism, woman was freshly degraded in Germany, in spite of the relatively high achievements of exceptional women, and for the sole reason that the mass of women were so far behind them.

But American men are not German men—at least not all of them. American men have been reared in the democratic tradition. It is my conviction, based on observation and conversation and experience, that the more intelligent an American man is, the more troubled he is by the present relationship between man and woman. He would like to have woman more intelligent and more responsible, but he does not know how to get her to want to be.

I happened to be sitting at dinner, one night in Washington, next to an unusually intelligent Congressman.. He said, as we talked of this: "The truth is we give women what they think they want. They want to be babied, so we baby them."

The depth of contempt in his voice, of which I am sure he was unconscious, made me cringe.

But what he said was true. American women can have what they want. It is not man who keeps woman where she is in our country, but herself. Yet whatever the cause, she has now come to a place where she is helpless unless man helps her. And the way he can help her is by demanding more of her. And where he must demand more of her is first and most in the home. Any American man who marries a vigorous, alert, well-educated girl—a girl eager and anxious to make a success of herself and of wifehood and motherhood—and lets her become the average woman she too often becomes is equally to blame with her. For woman is pathetically eager for man's approval and, far more than she should, she patterns herself to his wish. I do not excuse man in his vanity about supporting his wife and paying all the bills, in degenerating too often into sulkiness and irritability from fear of what people will think of him if she works outside the home, in giving so little of his real self to his marriage and his home. Man seldom helps woman. He is lacking in responsibility toward marriage itself.

And yet now he must help woman. It has suddenly become urgent that he do so, for unless he does he will lose woman altogether in the slave she will become—and has become when democracy changes overnight into fascism. The real threat to democracy lies in the way men think about women, in their ignorance of her true female nature, in their carelessness of her development, in their contempt of her great abilities, in their ignorance of her much-needed, and still almost entirely lacking, influence in the affairs of nation and world—an influence which, if it were there, would supply the balance which we have not now. Until woman contributes her share to life, we shall not find the balance which will conserve life and improve life conditions. Only this balance can provide the true foundations for peace. We shall have no peace until men and women work together outside as well as inside the home, not because either is superior but because life is designed on that balance and evil results when the balance between the sexes is lost.

I might, in discussing this matter of the man, woman and child in their relationships as individuals and as a unit in the home, bring to your attention many incidents and examples and issues. I have chosen rather to go to what I consider the deepest source of all the problems of adjustment between these three. It is a pulling and hauling between national ages, the medievalism of women and the modernity of man. Between them is the child, emotionally pulled back by the mother, intellectually hauled forward by the father. How can we expect him to be a harmonious being? The average young American is not harmonious in himself. He is dazed, uncertain whether to be progressive or reactionary, his fine character and true idealism destroyed by this uncertainty, and he is bewildered as to its causes. And, within her own self, woman is both medieval and modern and thus torn again. She is educated to be modern and then is put back into traditional life. And man is full of impatience with her, not understanding why or what is the matter with her or what it is in God's name she wants when it seems to him he is a sacrifice already to her whims—as too often indeed he is. He must realize that she does not know what she wants and he has to open her eyes to herself.

Yet how can he? All of his education has been away from her and not toward her or for her, as it ought to have been. Men and women ought to be specifically educated for each other, to share each other's whole lives and so make life whole for both. We shall not achieve any sort of harmony between, and of, man and woman until we give them mutual knowledge of the world and of each other out of which real understanding can come.

I believe that boys and girls should be given the same body of knowledge as their mutual possession if men and women are to enjoy each other and be worthy of mutual respect as citizens of a democracy. Men should not be educated for work as a matter of course, and women for the home as a matter of course. Both should be educated for work and home alike. They should be given two kinds of knowledge, that which is asexual and common to both —such as the sciences and techniques of arts and professions and government—every sort of work. Then they should be given the fullest instruction about themselves, not separately but together. All that we know about men and women, their similarities and their unlikenesses, should be taught to boys and girls so that everything is common to them—all knowledge, all purpose, all possible equipment for life to be carried on together, not one inside and one outside the walls of a house. For what the world needs today is the work that women have not done in industrial development, in national government, in international relations. Men have clearly demonstrated that they have gone as far as they can without women outside the home. And within the home women have gone as far as they can without men.

The home we have now is an anachronism, a relic of pioneer times that are gone. It will be of less and less importance until men and women together bring every member of it into a living relation with the world outside. The true American home is yet to be evolved. It must be made again by man and woman working together, for woman can do no more as she is.

I do not for one moment mean to insinuate any silly notion that women are better or more capable than men or that without men they could have made any better job of the world than men have made without women. What I do say is that, without women, men have made a world in which technology is overdeveloped in comparison to human relations, in which force is admired rather than wise and humane controls, in which wars come in dismal repetition. And without man in the home, woman's life and work there become meaningless.

Obviously it is time for some sort of change. There must be mutuality between man and woman. They need each other fully. For men and women, alike in so much, equal in ability if not identical, are fundamentally different in their attitudes toward life. To woman, life is an achievement in itself, an end to be conserved. She alone knows the cost of producing life and of conserving it with her care. When it is destroyed through bad economic conditions or wars, her work is destroyed, her biological being negated. Her strongest instincts are toward the preservation of life and the bettering of its conditions.

And these very female instincts are what the world needs today. The fact that wars continue to break out in ever-increasing fury shows the complete lack of appreciation of life as an end worth having in itself. For this, women are responsible. By their continued retreat from those centers of energy where the affairs of the world are shaped and controlled, they have withdrawn from the world the possibilities of order, the betterment of conditions of human life and, above all, the possibility of peace. I believe, with whatever intelligence is mine, that until the constructive instinct toward life that is primarily woman's is fully employed—not in the narrow confines of her home but in the affairs of nation and internation—we shall have the sort of world we have today. Not because man is evil or woman good, but because unless men and women work together, their instincts cooperating and supplementing each other, we shall have an ill-balanced world full of maladjustments, individual and national, and therefore inevitably resulting in war.

For, though we do not understand it, the instinct of the male is toward violence and death. He seeks, strangely, to fulfill his being in destruction, even of himself. Psychology knows this but is not able to explain it. It may be that the deep roots of male animal instinct are still hidden in the human being, that instinct which so often ends the life of the male in the animal world when his function in begetting a new generation is over. The female must live on for more life, but the male is no longer needed. Out of this past, it may be, the human male carries a dark remembering of death. Or it may be that there is deep in men and women alike the need to be lost in some great sacrifice of self if the highest happiness is to be found. Few, I think none, can be fully happy without losing self in something. Women find this satisfaction in childbirth. They go down to death when a child is born, and self, biologically, is lost. But man has not that catharsis. His very begetting is an act for himself and not for another. And since he faces no death afterward, he creates a death of his own in struggle and disturbance and even war, in order that he may have this fulfillment of losing self.

I say we do not know what are the roots from which our instincts spring, or indeed what, in whole, our instincts are, or what they mean or how to use them well. But we do know that the death instinct must be balanced by the instinct for life or we shall have no life left. I believe that the condition in which humanity finds itself today is due directly to lack of balance between the instincts of man and woman, in the home first and then in the world.

Men and women of America must consider together how to build home again in this ever new and dangerous world. Men must no longer be irresponsible toward marriage and home, feeling their chief duty done by making financial support, and women must no longer be irresponsible toward that world where man lives, feeling her duty comprehended within the compass of four walls or at most a little community. The way of life we say we love and will die for has its roots very deep, and deepest and most secret of all—and the least seen and understood—is that great taproot of all life, the life of man and woman together, and with them, their child.

I I

To You on Your First Birthday

THIS is your day of independence.

Wherever you are, in whatever country you were born, this day when you are one year old is a big day for you and for your family, but especially for you.

Your mother and father are proud of you and also of themselves, for they have kept you alive for a whole year after they brought you into a tricky and troublesome world.

Your mother is proud because she has fought off illness for you, she has nourished you with food, she has tended your precious body; she has made mistakes but she has avoided catastrophe. You have not fallen out of the window, at least not dangerously; although you have striven to reach inaccessible spots in the house, outdoors, wherever you were left, yet she has appeared in time to save you or she has prevented you, even against your will. Although you have made every effort to fall out of bed, she has caught you in time, or if she has not, she has picked you up, mended the damages and consoled you with kissing or scolding, perhaps both. Some are kissing mothers and some are scolding mothers, but it is love just the same, and most mothers kiss and scold together. That will be your trial and your comfort as the years go on.

Your father, too, is proud of you. He sees you, not as the year-old baby who has kept him awake at night, who has certainly wakened too early in the morning, and whose most irritating habit is to absorb most of the attention of the one who is your mother but his wife.

This woman whom you share in common you feel belongs secretly and actually to you, especially if you are a boy. If you are a girl, the rivalry may be the other way, especially if you are born in the United States of America where fathers have a pleasant and unconquerable weakness for small daughters, whatever their age.

I once knew a grandmother who lived long enough to be several times a greatgrandmother—a robust, large, hearty woman of independent nature—and she said one day near the end of her life when she was thinking things over: "If I could live my life over again, I would wish never to weigh more than one hundred pounds. Then I would not have to do anything for myself—there would always be a man to do it for me."

I tell this true story merely in case you are a girl. It contains hidden advice. It is possible that even a boy might find something in it as time goes on.

At any rate, if you are a boy, your father shares your present delusion about your mother except he believes secretly and actually that your mother belongs first and most to him. You will have to fight that out as time goes on, and the end must be a compromise growing gradually weaker until you realize that it is time for you to find someone who belongs entirely to you. On that day, if you are a boy, your mother will shed private tears, but your father will say, "Well, it was worth it, but I am glad it is over. Now, my darling,"—your mother, not you, unless you are a girl—"we will have some time to ourselves." By that time you will not care, for not only will you be on the search but you will know that you have so consumed your mother that a part of her belongs to you forever, and no one can take her altogether away. However much she may be your father's wife, she is also forever your mother, and it depends upon her peculiar temperament as to which she will continue to be the most.

Your brothers and sisters and cousins, older than you or possibly nonexistent, are also proud of you on this, your first birthday. "Look," they will say—or perhaps they have already said—"our baby can creep, he can take two steps, he is almost walking—or he is walking—and he can feed himself and say six words."

They are measuring you by what they can do themselves, and the nearer you are to them, the prouder they are. Each one of them—if any exist—remembers that once he or she had to go through this slow process of getting to the hands and knees and then from the hands and knees to the feet and then, clinging to chairs and tables, to dare to let go for a moment or, most wonderful of all, to rise straight to the feet from the floor and stand, a mile high, to survey the world around. Each feels superior to you today and loves you the better for the feeling.

Grandfathers and grandmothers you may have, or you

may not, but it is better for you if you have them, for they
have learned lessons about babies that your mother and
father have not. They know that it is easier sometimes to
give you your own way than it is to compel you to such
dingy dishes as oatmeal or spinach puree, and that
cookies, though admittedly indigestible at your age, may
at times be digested with more nourishment than a cod-
dled egg served by force or even coaxing.

Grandparents have a secret sympathy with you because
they know much more than your parents do about you,
but you must not lean on this sympathy, for the first duty
of grandparents is to their children, who are your parents,
and not to their grandchildren, who are you. This is
prudent and reasonable, for they have to live with or near
their children, your parents, even if only spiritually, but
they reckon, sadly, that they will die before you have
come to the age of communion with them. They must, in
short, look to the buttered side of their bread, and so they
will often seem to desert you when you and they know
that your parents, and especially your mother, are doing
the wrong thing for you. Yes, you know it and they know
that you know it, but still they will not dare to come to
your aid. This sounds hypocritical, but when you are a
grandparent you will understand the predicament of the
aged.

Remember, if you can think of it, that though today it
seems impossible and you are not even interested in the
possibility, yet, if you can keep yourself alive with the
help of parents and friends and so pursue the course
called common, even you will pass through the usual

stages until the last, which is to be a grandparent. Only when you have reached that final development, will you be able to understand fully what it is to be one year old. Since your grandparents have reached the ultimate, they can and do understand you today, although you cannot understand them. Strange as it may seem while you gaze upon their wrinkled faces, so different from your round and rosy one, or if you grasp their dry old hands and find it is easy to keep pace with their slow steps, nevertheless they know what it is to be you, and they even retain within their hidden hearts certain childish traits. They are afraid of the coming night or, if not afraid, at least they wish to prolong the day, and they renew themselves in the understanding of you, and because of you they are even less afraid of the night, for they see, with your help, that life is a road which has no end, for it is always beginning. They take comfort in you and you take comfort in them, and that is right, for young and old are complete only when each knows and trusts the other.

Neighbors will be kind to you today, they will be polite, and when they are called in to admire, they will admire you. But you are not to take them seriously, for they will privately be thinking that they have superior children of their own, or if they have not, then they will feel envy for those who do possess you, and they will not love you the better for that. You will have to learn that most love is tinged with envy, and you will have to learn to accept love and envy alike, and be grateful for one and ignore the other.

In spite of all these people who love you and upon

whom you depend for life, please remember, however, that this day, your first birthday, is your day of independence. You have rights and they are inalienable ones. For your future benefit, in case somewhere along the way you lose them or never have secured them, let me tell you what they are as of today.

You have already learned an important truth, although you are only one year old. It is that you need family and friends, for if you are without them you die. This truth you must never forget. There will be times when you think you need no one, when in strength and pride you will declare yourself independent of everyone. But you will be wrong. The person who tries to live alone will not succeed as a human being. His heart withers if it does not answer another heart. His mind shrinks away if he hears only the echoes of his own thoughts and finds no other inspiration. When old age comes, his failing body, too, will make him afraid.

There is much in common between the very young and the very old, and they should not be separated. In the night, when you waken, you feel yourself solitary, you cry aloud, you stretch out your arms, searching for another human being. Your mother or your father comes quickly and you are comforted because there is someone near you. So must there always be someone as long as you live, and therefore you must cherish those who love you and you must send out your own love like a lantern to find those whom you can love, so that no one will be alone in the dark.

Did I not declare this to be your day of independence?

It is such a day and, even though you are now surrounded by love, do not be humble about it. You have rights, and first, above all, is your right to all the love there is. It is your right not only to have your mother's love, which you take as a matter of course, but it is your right to have love of some sort from everyone in your family and your neighborhood, even perfect strangers. You may be naturally lovable, that is, you may be a tidy child, a child with a quick and bright smile—a wonderful gift and one even more useful, in the long run we call life, than good looks or talents. Anything that makes people love you is an asset, and the gift of smiling easily will outlast your present softness of flesh and roundness of limb and such attributes as make people of a demonstrative nature wish to pick you up and hug you.

Please allow people presently to hug you, insofar as it is supportable. The desire does not last. You will grow leggy, your teeth will drop out, you will cease to be a baby, and people will cease then to wish to hug you. But if you repulse them now, they will not forgive you.

I once knew a small, yellow-haired, blue-eyed baby boy who, because of his fatness and amiability, no one could resist. Involuntarily, people hugged him or wished to do so. As soon as he could speak, he cried out "No—no!" and so severely that adults were compelled to subdue their impulses. Today, although he is six feet tall, a bony, hairy young man whom only a very limited number of persons might wish to embrace, yet those who remember him as a one-year-old child feel a rankling hostility to him still. He is suspected of an unloving heart. The moral of this is, enjoy all the love that is offered you as long as you are a baby.

Allied to the gift of winning love is the kindness of disposition which allows people to love you. There are babies, mostly boys, to be sure, who, even as early as the first birthday, avoid love if possible and when they see a looming hug or hear a prattle of adult baby talk, they resist by stiffening the backbone or lunging out with the fists and feet or merely by a cold and blank stare. The fortunate babies of your age, also the wise ones, will not so behave. They will suffer others to love them, knowing by instinct that there is nothing the human heart longs so much to do as to love someone—almost anyone in fact— and that the power to love is one of the first to be lost. Remember this, please, while I speak of independence. For if you teach yourself to suffer the loving to come unto you, love, too, will be your comfort someday when you know better than to take it for granted, as you do now.

You have other rights besides the right to love and be loved. You have the right to grow at your own pace. This is very important, and in your enjoyment of love or your fear of scolding, I hope you will not allow yourself to be hurried through life. You have had a good deal of velvet-gloved compulsion during this first year, you have been propelled more than you know, but now that you are a year old, please insist upon growing at your own rate. Do not allow your anxious and fond parents and brothers and sisters to force you to utter so much as one word earlier than you wish to utter it, and do not take a step before you do so from your own desire. All your life long there will be people who want to hustle you, to measure you against standards that other hustled persons have set, to condemn you for not hustling. Today, on your first birthday, take the stand of permanent independence. Walk when you wish to go forward on your own feet, speak when you have something to say, play with the toy which stimulates your interest, whatever that toy may be and wherever you find it.

Above all, demand your independence in the matter of food. Eat only what you like, when you like, and as little or as much as you wish. You will have to be firm about this, for in many mothers there is a curious, inverted love which makes them desire passionately to stuff their children with a variety of inedible but nourishing foods. They believe that they are doing this out of pure love and the desire to see you get fat. The desire to see you fat and well-grown for your age is real enough but the motive may be questioned. If you are fat, you are a credit to your mother and when she wheels you about the neighborhood in your coach, she can compare you with other smaller, thinner children and can take pride in her motherhood. While it is innocent perhaps to wish to show oneself as a successful mother, the true test is not whether you are fat but whether you are happy and healthy.

Happiness and health, as you well know, depend upon eating no more than you wish at any time and eating, moreover, what you like and only when you are hungry. A sensible mother will not, of course, allow you to see or to taste actually harmful foods, and therefore you will not know you like them. But it is difficult for all one-year-olds

to persuade mothers to let them judge the capacity of
their own stomachs and the peculiarities of their own likes
and dislikes. Do not be discouraged. Keep up your normal
and justified methods of protest. Spit out of your mouth
what you wish not to eat, or set your teeth and refuse to
open your mouth at all. If extreme measures are necessary, scream and throw the dish on the floor. Mothers do
learn by such methods, or at least they give up.

Be yourself, in short. Like all human beings, you were
born with the silver spoon of supreme self-confidence. You
cried when you felt like it; you ate or did not eat. I hope
that during this first year of your life they have not dried
that source of all creation, yourself, whoever they may be.
I hope you still cry when you feel like it, for it is important to be able to cry. Later you may lose the power of
tears and then your dry heart will ache. Cry, therefore,
whenever you feel the need, and cry until you are cried
out and refreshed and able to smile again. Do not heed the
efforts of those who would stop your tears, even out of
mistaken kindness. It is not only your right to cry, but
it is good for you to cry. If your crying irritates others, it is
merely because they cannot cry, although they would like
to do so, lifting up their voices as you still do without
shame and letting their tears run down their cheeks. The
last thing you must learn is shame, and better if you never
learn it.

There are, it is true, many shameful acts in life, and it is
inevitable that you will commit some of them. When you
do you must be sensibly ashamed, and the test of what is
shameful is this—Did you know better? If so, and you

denied your knowledge, for your soul's sake be ashamed and wash yourself clean in your shame and then forget it, except as a determination not to be foolish again. For the fruit of good and healthy shame is the determination to be different. But this has nothing to do, actually, with you on this your first birthday. It is only a foretaste of what you will have to face later on.

Speak only when words come from you of their own accord. Smile when you are coaxed, but think about something else and do not yield. If your legs are weak, do not struggle to take steps, even though you are suspended by the hands from your father's forefingers. Crumple your legs and sit down on the floor and do not indulge his false pride in you. Wait and let him wait until one morning when you are feeling unusually well and happy, and your health and happiness will then run through your veins with your blood, and your legs will stand up of their own accord. Then soon you will walk all the time, and then, with the perversity of parents, your mother will cry out because you are into everything, but remember that it is your right to get into everything, for this is the way you learn.

The next right that you must declare on this your day of independence is the right to learn where and when you can. It is the business of your parents to keep you alive in this process of learning. It is their responsibility, not yours, to keep your fingers out of the electric outlets, lest you be instantly dead, and they must watch you while you climb the stairs, following you step by step so that when in the flush of pride you reach the top and turn for their approval, which you deserve, you may not fall backward and break your bones. Your bones are not your business yet. It is strictly the duty of others to guard you but not to hinder you. Your duty as well as your joy now is self-education. Never again in any years of your life will you learn so much and so well as you have learned in this year and will learn in the next.

Your best teacher is yourself, and this will always be true. No one, indeed, can teach you anything unless you want to be taught. Schoolteachers will discover this even later than your parents, though it will take them years to learn it and some of them never learn it. You know it already. You are your own best pupil just as you are your own best teacher. I hope your parents know this, too, but if they do, it is most unusual and you are a fortunate child. You will do well in life, you will grow up adjusted, as they call it, and you will not have to pay money to psychiatrists. If your parents do not know it—and this is more likely—then you are beginning a long struggle and you can hardly hope to escape damage, for if you yield to them, you will become a weakling, at the mercy of any strong-armed bully and dictator, and if you rebel, you will get the habit of rebellion which may end, if you are stubborn enough, in your becoming the sort of person who rebels at everything and one who will eventually pull down the walls of a nation as Samson pulled down the walls of the temple to his own destruction and the destruction of all within.

There is the possibility that you have parents of good sense who will learn from you as they strive to make you learn from them. If they are indeed persons of good sense, they will reason with each other and later with you, and you will all arrive at a state of compromise. That is, you will grant that in some ways they know better than you. As, for example, when you try to drink a bottle of liquid of a pleasant color, labeled POISON, you will grant that they have the right to forbid it. The state of compromise means that each of you allows to the other certain inalienable rights: you to have all freedom short of killing yourself or others; and they the right to forbid you dangerous pursuits which would end in death or injury for yourself or others.

This is enough for the first year. Independence takes on subtler aspects as time goes on, and your second birthday will certainly present more complex rights, that is, rights more entangled with those of other people than this first birthday reveals.

Today is yours. Take your own pace, talk when you must, walk when you like, cry as you please, ignore the boring, but smile at least as often as you can for those who love you and for the stranger who longs to love. Feel no duty toward keeping your diapers dry, and when you sit in your high chair with the bowl of porridge before you—or better still, the soft-boiled egg—ladle it into the air if you feel inclined. Now is the time to do that sort of thing, for later the rights of others and their reluctance to clean up after you may make it harder for you or even prevent you. This is the age of freedom, the age of being one year old.

ON WOMAN'S ROLE

12

Women, a Minority Group

ANYONE who belongs to what is commonly called a minority has a great deal to think about today. Every minority is face to face with the old question of what to do. Shall it join other minorities in a temporary union, hoping to find mutual benefit in combined strength, or shall it remain aloof from them and be compelled perhaps to accept subjugation under an uncongenial power? Neither answer will give complete satisfaction because both carry compulsions. A union between minorities may be as disastrous to them individually as a subjugation. The superficial, the impetuous, the impatient, will refuse to believe this, but it has been found upon experience to be true.

Who are the minorities? They are to be found as nations and as groups within nations. The main point is they are not static, neither by nation nor by race nor by groups. Thus, nations which today are minorities may once have been great powers—Portugal, for example, and the Netherlands. Today's great powers may one day be minorities. Nor is there any one race which has been permanently a minority. The Japanese were certainly once an Oriental minority, but now no more, if the criterion is power. Negroes in one part of the world may consider themselves a minority; in other parts of the world they are not.

There has been only one permanent minority group without limit of nation and race and it is made up of all women. Women in every nation have been in history, and are still today, the largest and the most real minority group. Even in the United States where they have had the most freedom, they remain the largest minority group, far exceeding in number and in lack of equality any other. The centenary of their struggle for equality with other groups has passed the century mark, but not with any sense of achievement completed. Within more than one hundred years, this minority group has with infinite pains secured, in the United States, rights given freely to male citizens; the right to possess property and to make wills; to speak in public meetings; to receive education equal to men's and to obtain degrees; to be eligible for government offices, to enter professions and be paid a wage equal to man's; to vote and to assume the privileges and responsibilities of citizenhood.

Yet women maintained a long struggle against more than a thousand laws in various states discriminating against them as a sex. They struggled, and until only recently without apparent success, for the right to have the Constitution of the United States apply to them in the same way as it applies to men. They must still struggle against prejudice toward married women workers, against prejudice toward women in the professions, in business, in government, and to some extent in the arts. They continue, therefore, as a minority group, even in the free and democratic United States, for years, perhaps generations, to come. And if this is true here, it is more so in other countries. And let American Negro men, when they feel inclined to anger and self-pity for the Negro as a minority, remember that women of all races in our democracy, the United States, were forced to stand aside in their struggle for enfranchisement while Negro men were given the vote. The Nineteenth Amendment was not ratified until 1919.

Women have always been, and are today, the world's greatest minority group, and they know it. There is no thinking, intelligent woman who in her heart does not know it and resent it and suffer under it. A few women have spoken out but most have not. Women, as a minority group in all countries, have gone on doing the work assigned to them and cooperating as far as they were able under restrictions in the life of those countries. They have not, as a group, gone on strikes or made revolutions. Their technique as they have become aware of their situation has been to perform their tasks while they struggle to better themselves and to remove inequalities based on the mere accident of birth. For it is as much chance and accident that a human being is born a woman instead of a man as that one is born white or black or yellow; and discrimination based upon such accident is as cruel and unjust for the woman as it is when it is based upon the accident of race.

I call attention to women as a minority group among other minority groups merely because it should be remembered, now when there is so much talk about minorities in the world, that women are the largest minority group, in numbers as well as in the massed inequality and prejudices under which they must pass their lives.

I advocate no violent action about this fact, no clamor or resentment, certainly no revolution, for I believe that no permanent good is achieved by such methods. I have seen revolutions within a country more than once, and seen them from start to finish. I never saw a revolution that did not leave people debased and conditions worse than before. I believe that the women progressing as a minority struggling for equality has been the right way. When women have gone on working while they pressed steadily for their rights, they have put each forward step upon the solid foundation of worth. Women have deserved each right as they claimed it. That they will achieve what they desire is sure because development has preceded the attainment of each right. It is a method which minority groups everywhere will do well to consider in their present doubts.

13

The Education of Women

IN A SUBJECT so large I have wandered here and there, trying to choose what to say about the education of women. I could easily choose a single aspect such as, for example, the choice of subjects which a woman's college should offer to its students. Or I could choose one subject, such as literature or the art of writing, and still hardly penetrate a surface. Instead, I choose to plunge straight into the basic problem that women face before, during and after such education as they get.

It is comprehended in three questions pertinent to us all. Before we can know how to educate women, we must, as women and teachers of women, ask ourselves where women are in relation to time and what women are and what they should be educated for. Any curriculum that is not founded upon the answers to these questions, or failing answers, even upon the questions, must fail to that extent in truly educating women.

First, let us ask ourselves where women are today and, since I am an American, allow me to try to discover where American women are. The answer to this question can be found succinctly expressed in a small, significant book written by a small, significant woman. The book is *Gift from the Sea;* the woman is Anne Lindbergh. Still another significance, and the greatest of all, is the fact that when it appeared this book went to the top of the best-seller nonfiction list and continued there, off and on, for many months. Most of the readers of books are women. Few men have time to read—they say—beyond the specific demands of their jobs and their sports. So it is women who read this book, millions of women. Nearly all women liked it. All housebound women liked it, almost without exception. The few I heard who questioned its worth were career women, usually unmarried or having married late. They said, in effect, "What is Anne Lindbergh complaining about? She has everything." It is true. Anne Lindbergh does have everything, and yet apparently it is not enough.

Most American women, almost, have everything, and evidently it is not enough or they would not have found in this book such a welcome expression of their own needs. The significance of this book therefore is not in what it says, for what it says is not profound, or in the way it is said, although it is written with grace and poetry. The significance is that what Anne Lindbergh feels is what most American women feel, and what she feels is dissatisfaction with herself and her life. Here is a woman who has wealth enough so that she is not oppressed by housework. Here is a woman beautifully educated and with access to all the treasures of art and civilization in her own country and abroad. Here is a woman who has made an apparently happy marriage and has a family of fine children. She has known tragedy, but who has not, on the way to maturity? Yet she is so dissatisfied that she flees her home to find a brief solitude by the sea and there tries to compose herself to return to her life. Her life is not *herself*. It is a battle which she wages every day. It is not a means through which she lives, for if it were, she would not fly from it, alone, or need to compose herself. She would be composed by life and through its daily living. And as she finds herself, so millions of American women see themselves in what she writes. They are unsure of themselves, they are divided, they are not ordered personalities. And, it seems, the more educated they are in the formal sense, the more divided they are within.

A few years ago I heard an American woman put into one trenchant sentence the whole problem. She said, "Why doesn't somebody tell us what we are supposed to be so we can be it?"

My answer to that question was, I now know, quite superficial. I said, "Why should you ask anyone what you are supposed to be? Why not decide what you want to be and be it?"

I know now that such an answer was useless. The woman—and most women—do not know what they are really supposed to be. So they do not know where they are or what is their relation to the other half of the human race, man—or even to the whole human race. They cannot understand themselves any more than Anne Lindbergh has understood herself. They grapple with the immediate problems of everyday, are fairly successful,

and yet their success brings no peace and joy. Anne
Lindbergh, the artist, the creator, longs for wholeness.
Anne Lindbergh, the wife, the mother, longs for wholeness. Neither woman is whole in her, and both being only
partial, she is divided irreconcilably in two. And this is
the predicament of the American woman, and so far her
education has done nothing to make her whole again.
There is not one career woman who, I believe, if she is
married and has children, is free of a secret sense of guilt
lest she has not been a good mother, and few are the
wives and mothers who are content to be only what they
are. And so millions of women read *Gift from the Sea*
because they felt they were reading about themselves.

This is the basic problem of women, all women, and it
is the problem which the teachers of women must face.
How far, they must ask themselves, does their teaching go
toward mending this split in woman's nature? Until it is
mended, we shall not have what the world so sorely lacks
today, the power and the influence of women, freely
expressed and used without shame or subterfuge, and
beyond that, valued equally and universally with the
power and influence of men.

How shall we mend this split personality which is
today's woman—certainly today's American woman? I
think first of all by assuring her that she has no reason for
guilt. Her uneasiness, her self-doubt, her bewilderment,
are not the result of her own wrongdoing or failure. Indeed, her accomplishment is extraordinary. She is not only
housekeeper, mother, wife, she carries on in her spare

time the civic works upon which much of the nation's welfare depends.

Few men have, or think they have, time for good works. Yet good works abound in every village and town. Women are, however, not only the mothers but the teachers of children. Their occupation is unlimited in scope and variety. They are in no sense failures except that they feel they are, and that they feel they are is because of a deep, vague but strong conviction that they have no real hand in the direction of human destiny, no power in the government of human affairs. It is true. They have not. That place, which in early human history they had, they have lost. That they may regain their share in the control of life, they must be taught that they are not, individually or generally, responsible for their decline. They must understand that woman is still in the downward sweep of man's ascendancy, and man's ascendancy began when he discovered he was an essential factor in creation.

How did this decline of woman, this ascendancy of man, come about? It began in the very beginning of human time. Ages ago, when there was no family, when man was a playboy running through jungles in packs, hunting big game, woman found herself in a strange and curious predicament. She discovered she was not man or like man, and this because of a visitation upon her body. Once a year, usually in the spring when the sun came back to the north and warmth spread over the land, she noticed that her breasts swelled; then, later, that she felt something move within her that was not herself. Soon, within a measurable time, a child came from her body. If it were a male, he grew up and joined the playboys. If it were a female, she in turn, when she was sufficiently grown, went through the strange experience when the sun came back in the spring. Neither man nor woman connected this experience with a sort of madness which overtook man at certain seasons. Early man had a rutting period, as other animals do, lasting about a month. The rest of the year his instincts were quiescent. Woman shared in this period. But she did not connect this game with what happened to her afterward, because many days passed after man had returned to his forest play before she felt the swelling of her breasts.

Then woman began to think. She struggled to understand why the experience was hers alone. Who put the child in her? How did it get there? Her brain developed because she thought. Women in those days lived in tribal camps together, nurturing their children and thinking and wondering and later perhaps talking together; their brains grew far more than did the brains of the males, wandering solitary, without the necessity for thought, in their forest lives.

Today we know that the sutures of the brain case in the male, as a species, close much earlier than do the brain sutures of the female, which means that man ceases to develop earlier mentally than woman does. Her brain continues to enlarge after his does not. In phylogenetic terms, this means that the female has been mentally active over a longer period in human history than has the male. He began to develop his brain late because he had only himself to think of, whereas the woman had the wonderment of her being, which yearly in the spring, through all the middle portion of her life, created another being from her own.

She was therefore compelled to become a reasoning being, asking the cause of the result she saw. The Aristotelian dialectic has its birth in this early wonder of the woman observing her own body which, in some way she did not comprehend, was possessed by a force outside herself. Quite naturally, then, she connected this annual change with the sun. From the sun, she reasoned, putting two and two together, came some sort of power that descended into her body. There must be a goddess in the sun, a powerful being who sent a force. But how? That was the next question. Again woman put two and two together. The birds came back in the spring, with the sun. The birds could fly high into the sky. They were like stars in the sky, and indeed stars and birds were thought to be the same. It was they who were the messengers of the sun. The birds were divine. With their song and their presence, they brought down power to woman's breasts, and so new life was created in her.

I cannot here take time to describe—or perhaps only to remind you, for what I have written may be already familiar to you—the effect of this explanation of woman's generative gift. She felt herself possessed by a heavenly power. She was in communion with divine being, she and she alone. Man had no part in it. She began to evolve at a rapid rate. The bird cries she began to consider meaningful, and language was born. Bird marks were the first written language. Woman, still thinking, believed that the birds, with sounds and marks, brought direct messages from the Sun Goddess. The primitive root sounds of all languages are founded upon the songs and cries of birds. As language developed, all names of objects were feminine in gender, although gender did not develop, as such, until the relativity of male and female was understood. Chinese, which is the oldest as well as the best preserved monosyllabic language system, is certainly based upon bird marks, as Chinese scholars have always declared. Woman, evolving language, thus evolved a means of communication with the Sun Goddess.

In this communication, again, she was alone. Man had nothing to do with it. But man, as her child, learned of her knowledge in which he had no part and he came to look upon her as teacher and wise one. I may in passing only ask your attention, for the moment, to the persistence of the bird into symbolism, even of the present. The dove of peace, the Holy Spirit descending as a dove, the stork that brings the baby, are only a few examples. Undoubtedly, too, the many stories in any literature of women divinely impregnated are remnants of the matristic era.

Woman was therefore the ascendant sex. Man served her as his mother. He enjoyed her as his partner in sex play. He revered her as the one who knew what he did not, the one who communicated with the divine Sun Goddess. Above all, she was the one, the only one, who could create human beings, even males like himself. It did not occur to him that he had any creative power whatever. Consequently woman's power over him was absolute. He was even forbidden the use of language except for words such as food. Man was woman's servant but also pupil. He hunted to find food for her and her children. He did not reason and his thinking powers were small. He needed only brute strength to bring home the meat and do the hard work. The first society was undoubtedly a matriarchy of the purest sort.

The caveman, dragging home his woman by the hair, is a late invention of a patristic age. It probably had no reality in fact. By the time man began to have an inkling of the relationship between his sex madness and a child born later of woman, he was no longer caveman and she was no longer cavewoman. They were well advanced in a civilization whose creator and ruler was woman.

It is incredible but true that neither man nor woman discovered until comparatively late in human history that man shared in the creative process. Until the discovery was made, the matriarchy continued smoothly and over a long period. Woman's intuitive knowledge developed every aspect of her world. All political power was hers, all knowledge was hers. While remnants of the concept of the bird remained in the language—as for example the ancient Chinese root *Ku,* associated with bird and female in creation, or the associated syllable *fu,* also common in Chinese and denoting divinity and emanation and bird, and this same *fu* is related to the Greek root of the word physics, and to the German *Vogel*—but I must not wander into *this* fascinating path—woman came to believe that her creative power was self-generative, and that she needed no aid, even from the divine being. She thought she was self-fertilizing. This concept, however, she announced only when man had developed under her tutelage to the point of wonder about herself.

Conceive, if you can, a society based upon the principle, without conceit or arrogance, of woman as the superlative. If hers was the power and the wisdom, hers, too, was the responsibility for herself and man. She became, in the fullest sense, the ruler, political and ethical. She possessed and governed great city states and their vast wealth. Under her rule also were developed the sciences of logic, the basis of algebra. Philosophy and the arts flourished.

Somewhere in this time, a man, nourished by female learning, began to wonder, traitor that he was, whether he did not have something to do with this unique ability of the woman to generate and to create. He was jealous of her uniqueness. He, too, began to question. Why did he have the sex madness? Was it merely a game? If so, why did woman insist upon such careful preparation for the sex act itself? Actually, of course, this was designed to regulate his impulses but she did not tell him so. And what, he wondered next, was the emanation from him? Was there not something divine in the nervous energy of the final moment? Did he not also possess a sort of milk like that which the woman secreted so sacredly in her breasts? Could the emanation from him be divine in itself?

The perils of education were realized. The pupil began to wonder. He began to question his teacher. At this fatal point woman took alarm. If man began to wonder and to question, as she had done, she was threatened. It was at this point that she eliminated the bird and the Sun Goddess and declared her own power of self-generation. Man at least could not produce a baby, an annoying fact which has continued to be true until this very day.

But, man argued—man the heretic—might he not have something to do with the baby? And if so, was not woman therefore dependent upon him to that extent? You can imagine the horror which this idea raised in the mind of woman. For thousands of years she had ruled supreme and ruled supremely well. She had founded civilization. She had taught man to gather and to build. She had decorated as well as devised. She had made music and painted pictures. Now her whole past as well as her present was shaken. The time in history was already late. The *idea* of male participation in the act of creation existed before the time of Plato, but Plato it was who nourished and brought about the fearful struggle between the Aristotelian logic of the relation of cause to effect and the male dialectic from effect to cause.

Bear in mind, if you please, the possibility that Aristotle was a woman, a concept which is accepted as a fact in the secret high places of European learning. She was at least an institutionalized matron whose words have been mutilated and partially destroyed, and yet who is known to have existed in some form as a personalized individual. Still, within the forms of matriarchal law and speech, Plato expounded his paternalistic heresy, not daring yet to be the open rebel and declare the era of man.

The long period of confusion which followed is not yet

ended and in it we find ourselves, men and women, imbued unconsciously with the attitude of enemies, and even while we fall in love with each other we are puzzled by our mutual inconsistencies. For woman, when she was matriarch and ruler, believed that because she created she should govern, and she did govern. When man therefore discovered his share in creation, declaring it preeminent, since without him woman could not create, he took woman's idea of the relativity between the power to create and the power to govern, and he assumed the role of ruler, or tried to, and is still trying to.

Confusion has followed, even in the languages. For the feminine roots have as yet been only partially replaced by the masculine, and gender remains, as the King of Siam said about the life in general, "a puzzlement." And confusion not only in language! For as the paternalists took over, and are still taking over, they have even meddled with history, changing dates and ancient books and essays to make it appear that men did what women actually did. Thus it is actually declared that Aristotle was the pupil of Plato instead of his teacher. But I need not go so far back for my example.

Let me mention an American woman, Anna Ella Carroll, daughter of a distinguished Maryland family. She lived less than a hundred years ago and was at her prime during the Civil War. A brilliant woman of fine ancestry, highly educated, skilled in the arts, she worked incessantly as a journalist to make money to keep her father's slaves from being sold. One by one, she bought them from him and maintained them somehow until the end of the war set them free. This, however, was only incidental to her work. She was an astute political writer, a thinker, a military strategist. Time will not allow me to mention her many achievements, but if you are interested you can read about her in a book, *Anna Ella Carroll and Abraham Lincoln,* by Sydney Greenbie and Marjorie Barstow Greenbie. I choose only one incident to illustrate my point.

At a moment in the Civil War when the Union forces were in meditation a plan to fight down the Mississippi River was found to be impractical. The current was too swift for boats to retreat if necessary, and the banks of the river were heavily fortified by the Confederate forces. Frontal attack was dangerous. The loss in men and boats would be too severe.

Anne, as she was called, was pondering the map one gray November day. "Everything," she wrote later, "seemed to hinge on the ability of our forces to fight their way down the strongly fortified banks of the river."

Suddenly, after a moment's reflective prayer, she glanced again at the map. She saw what she had not seen before. The Tennessee River flowed the other way! By it, one could take the fortresses from their exposed backs, cut the Memphis and Charleston Railroad, and get through to Mobile. It was the wedge through to the South for which the Union forces had been searching. She wrote a note to Attorney General Bates and to Thomas Scott, outlining her idea, and then she wrote to Lincoln. Her plan was adopted and followed with entire success. A century has passed, almost, and a student of military strategy has tried to explain Lincoln's sudden emergence as a war leader. For at a certain moment Lincoln, who had been floundering among his generals—none of whom knew what to do—suddenly rose to his feet and told them what to do. That moment coincides with the time when Anna Ella Carroll presented him with her plan.

The two weeks following this event, Anna Ella Carroll spent in writing a document entitled *"War Powers of the General Government."* She finished it and took it to the printer to be published.

Here I quote the authors of the book I have mentioned:

Nothing since the Declaration of Independence has so entered into the fabric of American political thought or been so potent to determine national action in moments of supreme crisis as this document . . . It was written to establish Lincoln's right to assume powers implied but not directly conferred in the Constitution. Into this little book of seventy pages, defining what Lincoln might and might not do in this national emergency, she [Anna Ella Carroll] distilled the essence of three centuries of unremitting battle for freedom within the framework of universal moral law. It became the official directive of the Lincoln administration in dealing with the unprecedented conditions of civil war.

Well, the upshot of all this—and I have mentioned only two among many events for which this woman was responsible—was that the moment came when someone had to be rewarded. A general must be chosen for hero. He had to be named. Lobbies vied with one another for the favorite general. A strategy meeting was called by a Mr. Wade at the home of Secretary Chase, to settle the choice.

When Anna came in everyone looked at her with embarrassment. They were all men.

Then Wade said something like this: "Miss Carroll, you have the whole Army to fight. The truth is known. They will be better in opposing you than in fighting the enemy."

She said, "For the time being no one must know. The President must not be embarrassed."

When the President, Mr. Lincoln himself, came in, he said, "Could I dare to let it be known that the armies of the United States are moving under the directing hand of a woman?"

"I am afraid not," Anna said. "Not in the present depressed state of women. Someday we may free women as well as slaves."

So ends my example. What I want to say to women and teachers of women is that the problem Anna lived with—of having always to swim under water, so to speak, of having to do work for which men are paid and recognized—is still the problem of woman in this patristic age, an age which is the unfinished rebellion, defined two thousand and more years ago by Plato, of the male against the female. Man is still not secure enough in himself to grant woman credit for her share in the creation of life. He has not yet forgiven her for the long centuries in which, in all innocence, she believed herself to be supreme and his superior. Woman is still living in the age of man's vengeance. Having escaped from serfdom to woman, man dares not let her rise to be his equal lest her abilities, once so powerful, emerge again. He does not forget that once she even declared that she alone com-

muned with the gods. And woman has not yet recovered
from the shock of her displacement. She is still bewildered
by her fall.

Well, what has all this to do with the education of
women? It has everything to do with it. For unless and
until woman understands why she is in the position in
which she finds herself today, all the education in specific
subjects that she may be given will not help her to
understand herself and man. I submit that the purpose of
education is to help woman and man to understand each
other. Only then can balance, or as we call it, peace, be
restored to the world.

A state of imbalance between the two basic groups of
human society results in a state of irritation, a pervading
melancholy which colors every activity in life. Today the
imbalance results in a world given over to warlike proce-
dure. Man, proceeding alone, as he does now, continues in
his natural state of war and strife. That is his forest
inhʳritance. Only woman, working equally with him in
affairs, can bring balance. One hears it said that women's
vote has brought very little change in our times. To which
the reply can only be that the vote is not enough. There
has to be the basic change in education and opportunity
that will enable women to understand themselves in time
and function, for only then can they understand men.

Woman must be taught and convinced that it is not her
fault, or man's, that society is in imbalance. She must
understand that she acted in good faith when she en-
deavored to comprehend the early universe and when,
bewildered by the miracle in her being, she explained it as

best she could. She cannot be blamed that man seemed of less importance, for he was even more ignorant of the truth than she. And neither is at fault that their struggling brain stuff could not comprehend the truths of science. Woman, then, must not blame herself or man for anything. There is no guilt in either. If the feeling of guilt can be lifted, the air is cleared for the next step.

Woman must be shown and convinced of her own mental strength. She has been cowed and humbled and her submerged sense of injustice at the hands of man has burst forth or crept forth in demeaning ways. But she is still wrong to blame man. He, too, needs the same education. He must be taught not to blame woman. She is innocent of oppressing him, and he must cease his revenge against her for ages past. These are the deep truths which must be taught.

Woman must learn all that man learns, in order that her opportunity may be equal to his. She must receive equal recognition and recompense for her equality. Man must be taught that it demeans him and lessens his stature when he is not willing for woman to be rewarded and recompensed. Woman must, by her steadfast excellence in mental as well as physical performance, convince him and with determination. She must first persuade and then demand. Where he will not allow, we must remember that it is not as easy for men to be generous as it is for women, since they began late to celebrate and have not, besides, the hidden memory of divine communication.

We speak often of women's intuition. This is nothing but deep, unconscious memory of past wisdom. Left to themselves, men will not proceed far beyond where they are now. Indeed, they will pursue their patristic way until the world is destroyed. Woman must come forward in time to save, not because she is the savior, but because she alone provides the saving balance.

Do I mean to say that men and women, in education, should be the same because they are the same? Certainly not. They are not the same. I believe their education should be the same, in order that each may have the same advantage of knowledge, so that neither has secrets from the other. I think women should know all about men and men should know all about women.

Man and woman are very different beings. This difference penetrates to the last atom of body and brain cell. In their difference is the hope of the race. And since woman is traditional and historically wiser than man and more closely linked to the realities of the human group, her first task will be to understand herself and the reasons for her present state of mind. She must then understand man and the reasons for his need to insist upon himself as the ruler. She will have to convince him that he need not so insist because he need not fear her. She does not intend to return to her former place of power. Neither, however, does she wish man to be the dictator. She must remember how very recently man has discovered his own importance in the life scheme.

Therefore woman must not be made uneasy by certain men who inveigh against "Momism." These are adolescent rebels, and she can afford to laugh, to wait and work toward the reassurance of man, believing in full faith that when he is mature he will no longer fear her and her great gifts. The purpose of education is the reconciliation of woman to man and man to woman in the most complete and profound sense. Only then shall we see the fulfillment of the human being.

The teachers of women should encourage them to rediscover themselves in their noble past and, realizing their peculiar worth, to adjust their relation to man and to humanity today, with all the problems that confront us as a race, the chief problem being the fear that man still has of woman.

No less a person than Albert Einstein, in his work, *Cosmic Religion,* issued in 1931, said, on Page 105: "In Madame Curie I can see no more than a brilliant exception. Even if there were more women scientists of like caliber they would serve no argument against the fundamental weakness of the feminine organization."

Man's sense of inferiority is very deep indeed when he must so protect himself. Yet Madame Curie was not only the brilliant scientist but also the mother, the cook, the housekeeper, the protector of her husband, although in the part time that was left her she accomplished more than he.

It is this sort of inequality and negligence in recognition that woman must refuse to tolerate, not with anger or aggressive behavior but with dignity and firmness. She must not lend herself to competition, either with her sisters or with man. She must devote herself instead to solid personal achievement, as woman.

14

The Homemaker

O<small>N</small> a certain afternoon, well over half a century ago, a small girl sat sewing her daily seam with her mother. The small girl was I, the mother was mine. The seam I took as a matter of course, and it did not matter that I disliked sewing.

My mother's mother, of conservative French descent and Huguenot family, had reared her daughters to be good housewives, and this included, in that generation, the making of garments for the family. The garments were decorated with embroidery and lace, and these arts were taught, too. In due course, therefore, I had my seam to sew, embroidery to make, and lace to crochet. The same combination of plain work and artistic decoration also was necessary for cooking. I was taught to make bread as well as cake, to roast and broil and fry as well as to conjure up confections. A house must be thoroughly clean and ordered before flowers could be arranged, but all was equally essential to the well-being and happiness of family life. This work and decoration, my mother declared, was woman's business.

The afternoon was hot, I remember. Needle and thread and Chinese linen cloth were sticky in my fingers. I was rebellious.

"Suppose I don't want to be married?" I said.

"You need not be," my mother replied tranquilly. "Not every woman has to marry. But you must learn home-making for your own sake, whether you marry or not, because you are a woman. And—you will probably marry."

We were sitting on the veranda of our old mission house, and at that moment the gardener was sprinkling the flowers in the border by the compound wall. American homes in China always had these faithful servants; life there was dependent upon them.

"I shall have servants," I told my mother.

"Your servants will not respect you if you do not know how to teach them," my mother said in the same tranquil voice and, lifting her eyes from her own sewing, she smiled at me half mischievously. "You cannot escape being a woman," she said.

How true those words have been! Wherever I have been, whatever my work, I have not been able to escape being a woman, and deep in the heart of all women is the need to create a home. Not all women marry, perhaps today not all women can marry or even want to marry, and the home may be for themselves. Yet most women want to marry and do marry, and with marriage come the duty and the joy of creating a home, not only for one's self, but for others, too.

Let me say at once that I think it quite possible for

women to combine career and home. Indeed, today's high cost of living sometimes compels women to be wage earners as well as homekeepers. The combination is often difficult, especially during the years when children are small. I myself have been fortunate in being able to do my career work at home.

The room where I write is in my house and the door is always open to the children. I keep no hours which cannot be interrupted by my family. Work is not always continuous as a result, but I have learned to break off in the midst of an important chapter if child or husband needs attention. I have always put my family first. I am lucky, again, because this has been no sacrifice. It is necessary for a writer to live first if books are to have vitality, or so I believe; it is necessary for a woman writer, at any rate. Men are more remote from the sources and springs of life than women are. They may be able to spin out their stories in a human vacuum; women writers cannot. Those women whose books have endured have been women who literally wrote in the midst of the living room, surrounded by family, as Jane Austen did and as the Brontës did. I confess I am not quite so detached. I do have a room of my own, and must have it, as Virginia Woolff maintained. But the door is always open.

Well, what about the women who cannot work at home, who go forth to factory and business office every day? I see plenty of them here in my neighborhood nowadays. Ours was once a quiet rural county, a place of widespreading farms, of pastures, fields and meadows. All that is changed now, alas. A great steel company has moved into the lower end of the county where the Delaware River flows into the sea. Farms have been sold to become human anthills, and smoke is pouring out of chimneys, to blacken our once blue sky. Our women used to work placidly in comfortable stone farmhouses. Now they hurry out of ranch houses and split levels to sit at machines or in offices all day while the children are in school and the babies are in community nurseries or accumulate in the house of some stay-at-home elderly woman. Is all this necessary? It seems to be, as long as we want the latest houses complete with refrigerators, oil furnaces and the etceteras.

I was talking only the other day to a real estate agent about the sale of one of my own old farmhouses, no longer needed. It is a beautiful stone house, the floors of heavy oak board a century old, the window sills deep in the two-foot walls. I have modernized it enough to have a good well, bathroom and running water and an excellent hot-air furnace. It ought to sell for a good price but when I said so the agent looked rueful.

"Not nowadays," he said. "Only an elderly retired couple will want it. The young people insist on oil, everything automatic and modern."

For these new necessities women must pay as well as men. It is no longer possible for the man alone to bring in enough money. Yet were I an average young woman today, I would, I am sure, deliberately choose not to work outside my home even though it meant I had to do without the second car, the automatic furnace, and the pleasant extras. I would take what my husband was able

to earn, and with it create a home into which I could put
my life and creative skills.

Let us face the severe fact, however, that if woman is to
stay in the home—where she should be if she is married
and certainly if she has small children—then merchants
must understand there will be a drop in business. We
cannot maintain our present high purchasing power, we
the people, if income is held to the level of one person's
earning capacity. Economists will have to puzzle their
heads over this, and businessmen will have to realize that
they cannot eat their cake and have it, too. If the people
are to buy all the wonderful things that are made for them
to buy, if they are to yield to the seductive advertising
they see and hear every hour of the day and half the
night, then husband and wife will both have to bring in
the cash and woman cannot therefore afford to be homemaker alone. Such housekeeping as she does will have to
be hasty; her husband will have to help with the dishes,
the cleaning and the children. This is inescapable truth.
Perhaps man and woman will be the better for it—I do
not know.

Be this as it may, we must realize that homemaking, in
the full sense of the word and the deed, takes time. It
takes time, not only to do the actual work of keeping a
house clean and beautiful on limited means, but it takes
time to think about each member of the family in relation
to the home and to the whole. A woman cannot be hurried
and harried every moment of the day, struggling to earn
money and at the same time to be a real homemaker. She
knows she is not succeeding and she will, to silence her

own conscience, glorify the pleasure of having money to spend. Then the homemaker, the woman who does not earn wages in cash, listens and wonders in discontent whether she is choosing the right way. She is, she feels, nothing but a housewife.

It is to this woman, the homemaker, the housewife, that I address myself. It takes real self-discipline to be a good housewife, and not all housewives are homemakers. Some women put house ahead of home and then they are only cleaning women and cooks. Some women are lazy and cannot discipline themselves to do each day's work well enough to create a place of beauty and order for family life. It is very easy, when husband has gone to work and children to school, to settle down with another cup of coffee and the radio or television or even the telephone. The undisciplined woman in the home can cheat on the job, too, if she has no conscience. Home can be a place of escape from reality if a woman lets herself begin to slide. Women are as human as men and some people work only when they are watched. I suppose that such women had better go out to work where they can be watched and can bring back money, at least.

The real housewife, however, loves her home. Her house is only part of home. Home is the total environment and atmosphere in which the family lives. It includes the yard, the garden, the flowers on the table, the books in the living room, the music in the air, good talk as well as television, family excursions as well as indoor games on a winter's evening. The life shared by every member of the family with every other makes the atmosphere of home.

Beauty is essential and the foundation of beauty is order. The homemaker is responsible for beauty and therefore for order.

I am the last person in the world to insist upon a spotless house. Our living room can be thoroughly disorderly in the process of play or work, but when such periods are ended, I have always restored order. It is my duty to do so, as woman. Children have been taught to help, but when, in the natural rebellions of adolescence or in the haste of other demands, they do not help, then I restore order alone. It is my responsibility as homemaker, I believe, to keep our home as beautiful as I can without pressure on anyone, and there is no beauty without order. A room may be expensively furnished and tastefully designed, but if it is disorderly all values are destroyed.

Let me emphasize that order is not for order's sake but for beauty's sake. Order is the shape upon which beauty depends. A disorderly house is a disorderly home. A disorderly home produces disordered people. There is a clear relation between physical confusion and mental confusion.

Not far from where I live is a house I often pass as I come and go, but I never pass it without thinking of the story it hides. It is a pleasant house, neat and white, and the white curtains are crisp and fresh at every shining window. I have never entered it, but neighbors tell me that two men live there, father and son, and that the house is as neat and pleasant inside as it is outside. They live alone, both men going to business in the morning and coming home at night. They did not always live there. The father bought the house some years ago, after his wife died. Before then they lived in a large old house a few hundred yards up the road.

"Why did they move?" I asked my neighbor.

"They wanted a real home," she said.

"And hadn't they a home?" I asked.

"No," she said. "His wife was a miserable housekeeper. Nothing was ever put away. A real lazy woman she was, though she hadn't nothing else to do. She gadded a lot, or she was on the telephone. When the man came home at night, the house was in a mess and she was behind with her work—always behind. He wasn't a talker—or maybe he quit talkin', I don't know. But when she died he sold the house, still in a mess as it was, and he bought the house he's in now and fixed it all up beautiful. Him and his son keep it clean and neat and they even keep flowers on the table. It's a real home, though there isn't a woman in it. It's beautiful."

I can understand that man. What his wife could not or would not create for him and their son, he has created. He has a home. I wonder sometimes why he hasn't married again, for he is a personable fellow, but I suppose he dares not risk another woman. She, too, might destroy his home. And my wonder is, why did his wife throw away her opportunity for happiness?

What work is greater for woman—or man—than the creation and maintaining of the center of human life, a home? Into this home children are born. It is their world, the only world they know for the most important years of their lives, and as long as they live it will continue the most important influence upon them.

Seldom indeed do men and women rise above the atmosphere of their childhood homes. They may become rich and powerful, they may build houses very different from the one they first knew, but they carry within themselves the atmosphere of the first home. If that home was a place of order and beauty, however simple, then they are tranquil and able to cope with life's problems. If there was neither order nor beauty in the home, the lack follows them all their lives. They may not know what is the matter with them or why they are eternally restless and seeking, but they know they live in uncertainty and inner confusion.

The relationship between the material and the spiritual—or, as Einstein put it, between matter and energy—is profound and real and its scope knows no boundaries. Indeed, we are only beginning to guess at its vast reality. I myself have always believed that spiritual grace flowers only from physical order and beauty. Sweet-tempered children grow easily in a pleasantly planned and well-ordered home. Irritable children and impatient, unhappy adults are the result, very often, of no more than the atmosphere in an unpleasant and disorderly house.

Woman, the housewife and homemaker, creates more than she knows. While she sweeps and cleans and makes the beds, while she cooks and washes and puts away, she is creating human beings. She is shaping dispositions and building character and making harmony. The greatest need in the world today is for people of sweet disposition, good character and tranquil, harmonious nature. It may be even internationally important for men to leave home in the morning, not only with the knowledge that their wives love them but also with the satisfaction of knowing they have orderly, pleasant homes from which to go and to which to return. I can believe, for example, that a delegate to the United Nations may take his place there in a frame of mind conducive to understanding and patience if he has emerged a few minutes before from a pleasant home whose beauty is based upon order.

The influence of woman, the homemaker, reaches indeed far beyond the walls of her house. Her reach is beyond her own comprehension. She creates the center where the world begins, the world and all its peoples. It is from her that they spring. As every human being, man and woman, emerges from her womb—and none can otherwise be born—so they emerge from the home she makes to receive them when they are born. True, man is her mate and cobuilder, but for some reason, perhaps divine, it is she who is the more responsible for the creation of life in all its forms.

There is something uniquely strong in woman. Seldom indeed can a man ruin a woman's life. She will make her life anew, again and again. She has an inner toughness that restores her to herself and to her function. But men are easily ruined by women. They are ruined in the home by bad mothers or bad wives. I say bad, because I believe a disorderly, lazy, selfish, incompetent homemaker is a bad woman. She has the most important job in the world, the most exciting opportunity, and if she does not perform it, she is not to be forgiven. If she is ignorant, then such ignorance is a crime because of the damage it does to the group of human beings for whom she is responsible.

Do I, who am a professional writer, believe that home-making is the most important work in the world for a woman? Yes, I do, and not only for others but for herself. As a writer, I know that it is essential for a woman to be a homemaker, and this is true whatever else she is. Insofar as she is a good homemaker, to that extent she will complete her own being. I will say, also, that to the extent that man is a successful husband and father, to that extent, too, he completes his being. Man and woman, we have our separate but cooperating functions to fulfill for our own completion, as well as for the human beings we serve because we are responsible for them. I know that it is necessary for me, if I am to work my best at my desk, to feel that around me is my home, ordered and as beautiful as I can make it. Home is my earth, where my roots are and from which I draw spiritual sustenance. Security itself is based upon this inner content.

The home, then, is the center of life. As the home is— the individual home, where one woman is the matrix—so the world will be. We have need, we women, as we survey our present world, to ask why it is so troubled. If we are honest, let us search back into cause and cure. I shall not be surprised if that search leads us home.

15

Men and Women

A QUARTER-CENTURY AGO, when I first came to the United States, my own country, to live and to make my permanent home, I was deeply interested in the American woman. My experience and training had acquainted me with the Asian woman, but I had known few Western women and none intimately. The American woman was new and exciting. She had a freedom to which I was not accustomed. She could come and go as she liked in city and country, even alone. She could go to school, to college, to work. At the same time she had an amazing amount of privilege. She need not work outside the home, she was treated with courtesy, and to a degree somewhat shocking to me, she was indulged by father and husband. She was excused from hard physical labor because she was a woman, and for the same reason little mental effort was expected of her. She was accustomed to being cared for.

The women of Asia are strong and independent. They have not had the advantages or disadvantages of tradition of chivalry, and they are not accustomed to being cared for. Their place in society was, and is, defined but powerful. In the family the woman was the de facto ruler, although she was trained to defer outwardly to her father, her husband or her elder brother. These men, although in authority, exercised it within the accepted limits and did not interfere with women in the home. When modern times provided the vote, women received it at the same time men did. In fact, in China, women had the vote before American women had it. Whatever deprivation Chinese women suffered in terms of illiteracy and lack of opportunity, men suffered it, too.

True, woman's place was in the home, but then the seat of power in Chinese society was the home. Unspoiled and without special privilege, the Asian woman did the practical work of life. She worked in the fields beside her husband and she stood behind the counter if he kept a shop. Men took it for granted that women worked wherever there was work to be done. In the present regime in China under the Communists, woman is expected to take her full place as a citizen, and now the effort is to get her out of the home. It is considered reprehensible that a woman should cook for one family or devote herself to the children of one family; if she wants to be a housewife, she should be cooking and caring for the children of many. Under Communism, men insist that women take full part in the industrial and cultural life of the nation, and they use ruthless means to accomplish the fact.

In the United States I found a paradox. The American woman had equal opportunity with man for education and training in the professions, but she did not utilize this education and training. Instead she married and went into a house and devoted herself to a small group, her own family. I hasten to say that I am all for marriage and home and children. Nor do I minimize the important role of woman as wife and mother. The question, however, was whether the woman was sufficiently or properly trained, even for this position, if it were to be her only one or, at best, her chief one. To educate her for mobility and freedom and then deny her that same mobility and freedom can lead only to frustration, and a frustrated woman is not a good wife and mother, however much she may love her husband and children.

I observed frustration in the American woman. She often repudiated the word, insisting that she wanted to be married, that nobody had forced marriage on her, that it was woman's highest calling, her natural place, and so forth. Nevertheless, in spite of such protestations, it was obvious that she was discontented in at least part of her being and most of the time. Her life was hectic between kitchen and school, her time schedule not her own but that of husband and children. To serve is beautiful, but only if it is done with joy and a whole heart and a free mind. The American woman served her family as a duty, brightened by love, it is true, and by intervals of joy, but the atmosphere she created in so doing was not one of continued content.

Out of these early observations I wrote a small book entitled *Of Men and Women*. This little effort has brought me thousands of letters from all over the world, from both men and women. Now, two decades later, I am often asked if I would write the same book again. My reply is

that I would, but I would add Part II. Much of what was
true a quarter of a century ago is still true. Woman's
education is the same, her frustrations are more obvious,
although some small attempt is being made to alleviate
her discontent, she is working outside the home to the
extent of supplying about one third of the labor force in
the whole country, but her basic situation remains the
same—with one great, notable, astounding difference:
Women have not changed, but men have changed.

Two decades ago the attitude of American men toward
women was tolerant but superior. It was still considered a
handicap to a man if his wife worked, a proof of his
incompetence—a man should be able to support his family. This is no longer true. A young man nowadays expects
his wife to help support the family if necessary. If it is not
necessary, he encourages her to work where her interest
leads her. This can only mean one thing—men have a new
estimate of what women can be and should be and—here
is the newness of it—in relation to themselves as men.

This change, which has only begun since the end of
World War II, is the result of several forces. Much is
being said about the emphasis on sex so apparent in our
literature, advertising and general culture. It is true that
this present emphasis is beyond reality, perhaps because
it is only the far swing of the pendulum from the past
when women were supposed to have little if any interest
in sex—"nice" women, that is. The other kind existed, of
course, but for men alone. The daring notion that women
enjoy sex as much as men do, if not always in the same
way, and the man's discovery that he himself enjoys sex

more when she does, has revolutionized the relationship between men and women as a whole. They have become partners, not only in reproduction but in the joy of creation.

Young husbands nowadays want to share more than the moment of conception. They share to a heartening degree the period of pregnancy, the hour of birth, the care of the infant, the growth of the child. Fathers are emerging from their unimportant and sometimes even ludicrous positions to a place of equality with their wives in this most delightful and eminently important function of producing the next generation. I do not say that all men so share, but the younger ones do share and want to share. That is important—they *want* to share. A real man, moreover, does not feel it threatens his masculinity to change a baby's diaper or to wash the dishes of an evening. It is only the man on the fringe of masculinity who fears that "woman's work" will change his sex.

This new interest in women which the American man is now evincing may have its beginning in a new appreciation of sex as a process, but it is developing into a new appreciation of woman as a human being. He does not now doubt her chastity or think the less of her because she, too, frankly enjoys sex. On the contrary, he is stirred to the depths of his own being; where he thought he was alone, he now knows he is not. Since she shares this basic need with him, he is the more inclined to share with her the other aspects of his life. He discovers that he likes to talk with her intelligently. He is impatient when her conversation is limited to trivialities and daily humdrum and gossip. Never before has the intelligent and well-educated woman had so much good male companionship as she has now. Even age does not prevent the attraction. I am impressed by the fact that while American men are hungry for a fuller companionship with women sexually, they are even more humgry for her companionship mentally and spiritually, too.

I wonder if American women realize this change in men. And if so, how many of them do? If they fail in such recognition, I fear for the world. For man, disappointed in woman, retreats into a frustration which can compel him to such cynicism and despair that he is capable of brutality on any scale, for which indeed she must assume responsibility. If American women can understand the opportunity they now have, and the responsibility, if they can accept both, they will enter upon a new life for themselves, one in which their freedom is absolute or as absolute as it can be in a world wracked by huge choices for good or evil. Even so, they may, if they will—if they can grow quickly enough—have a share in deciding what sort of a world it will be. Certainly the decision should not be left to men alone, as it still is as of this moment.

Yes, what I am saying is that nobody is holding women back except women themselves. The challenge that men give us today is simple and clear. They want women to be intelligent as well as beautiful. All the beauty aids in the world will not serve if the brain inside that carefully coiffed—or tousled—head is an empty one, vacuous and small. The instant's diversion will not last. Real men today want real women. Charm must be redefined. It must now include the delight of a mind alive and alert, thinking, imagining, considering, enjoying all that life can offer. Marriage is more than sex, more than home, more than family.

For the first time, at least in the United States, I discern in men a yearning desire for women who can fulfill them, and a yearning, equal in its intensity, to fulfill their women. They are beginning to find new depth in sex, new excitement in love, pervading the entire life and not limited to bed and board.

What a challenge this is to woman! How is she responding? Well, as of now, she is frightened. She is the more frightened, and even resentful, because women of other countries are entering her field. American men are marrying Asian women, European women—wherever they can find the women they need. The competition grows fierce. So far, American women are responding in terms of panic. They are catching their men very young.

I heard a young woman of my acquaintance complain only yesterday that "If you don't get married before you're twenty-two, your chances are slim. Someone else will grab him."

Crude, yes, but it accounts for many of our young marriages. The door of the house is wide open for woman to walk through it and into the world, but the stupendous scene beyond it terrifies her. She slams the door shut and pulls down the shades. She is so terrified that she sometimes even rails against the exceptional woman, the daring individual who accepts the invitation of the open door and enters into wider opportunity and assumes the new responsibility. Both fear and resentment are natural, though not intelligent. Every change into a new life is terrifying and seems impossible. A child at birth springs into the larger world beyond the womb, not with joy but with loud cries of rage and fright. When death draws near, the dread is deep. What change is this that strips from us the familiar body? We put it off as long as possible.

And—let us face it—women have had a good life and an easy one. Yes, yes, I know all about the hardships, the drudgery, the childbearing, the—everything! I maintain that it has been easy. The hardest work in the world is responsibility and men have had it, not women, with notable exceptions. Yes, yes, too, she has had to encourage the man and keep him at it and coax him and feed him food and love and sex in judicious amounts, but he is the one who has shouldered the responsibility and gone out of the open door. And she has stayed safely under the roof, knowing that he would return. Meanwhile, she gets the dishes washed and does the daily chores and keeps busy within her limits.

The trouble is that the limits must be removed. She must be busy with everything in the world and useful everywhere. If her housewifery prevents her development, then the plain truth is that woman must order her home duties. She must deal more efficiently with house-keeping demands. We would be loathe to allow our government to do what the Communists do—tell us sternly that the nation's work can no longer be done by man alone, that woman must help, and if she cannot organize her household work better, government will step in with communal kitchens and day nurseries so that women have nothing to do but work. I hear such rumblings already from men who feel the burden of today's world intolerable upon them, not only the actual labor but the heavier burden of intellectual effort in solving problems and devising new processes.

Women's brains are needed today in every field, in the highest echelons. Old prejudices are fading, intelligent men are eagerly seeking intelligence wherever it can be found, and they are impatient when intelligent women continue to live in narrow ways, apart from the world's problems and dangers. Now is the time for all good men, and women—

The demand is here, the opportunity waits. It is for women now to consider themselves and that open door. There is no household problem which, women working together, cannot be solved. The question which faces every woman is no longer—"Do I want to . . . ?" or "How can I . . . ?"

The answer is simple. You must! Man needs woman today as never before if the human race is to be saved. He needs her love and faith, yes, but he needs her actual cooperating work, both of hand and mind, and not only in the home and family. He needs her in every phase and level of national and international life and, most hopeful of all, he recognizes his need and is ready to acknowledge it.

> . . . Let me not to the marriage of true minds
> Admit impediment. . . .

True marriage is the complete cooperation of men and women together in all human life. To such mutual respect and responsibility let women not admit impediment. There are no impediments except in their reluctant minds. I believe that happy families and good children come only from true marriage between man and woman. Similarly and on a universal scale, a good society, a safe world, can come only when men and women work together, using their valuable differences and the special contributions of their individual personalities through comradeship and partnership in work for the human race.

OUR VALUES

16

The Pursuit of Happiness

I HAVE HAD and am still having a happy life. I think it is important to be happy. Life is not worth living when one is unhappy. That I learned long ago. The thing I had to learn was how to be happy. Yes, I had to learn it. It is really quite easy to be unhappy. The small details of daily life going awry can create such discontent that happiness is impossible. Then come the crashing disasters which overtake all of us sooner or later, and life is unendurable. Worst of all, perhaps, unhappiness may come out of discontent with ourselves, the way we look, our lack of talent, and the environment in which we find ourselves. How, then, shall we escape the inescapable?

First let me say that the most important lesson life has taught me is that happiness, or even contentment, has to be planned for and worked for if it is to be achieved. No one on earth or in heaven has promised happiness or even contentment to any of us. We are born without promises. We find ourselves here, enclosed in a body which was not of our making and which may be very different from the one we would like to have had, and belonging to a group

of persons, called a family, which may or may not be to
our liking, either. Yet each of us has certain talents and
potentials for happiness and each of us is given the instrument by which we may put them to use. This instrument
is the will. Some people use this instrument well and they
find contentment and consequent happiness of a very
permanent sort. Others never use the instrument, and
their lives sink into an habitual discontent that can only
result in permanent unhappiness.

What directs the will? It does not work alone. It is only
an instrument. It is the mind that directs the will. The
mind says, "This must be done if happiness is to follow."
For the will is a laggard. It likes to sleep. It prefers not to
exert itself unless compelled. The mind must compel.
Mind says, "I know this is what I must do, because it is
what I want to do for my own contentment." And mind
summons the will and insists upon performance. Will is
what makes you get up in the morning when mind says
there is work to be done. It is so easy to change night into
day by sitting up all hours doing nothing much. Then day
changes into night and nothing at all gets done. Discontent and unhappiness follow, since it is essential for the
human creature to do and to be. Mind, then, is the
planner, and will is the performer.

And in what area will the mind plan for contentment
and for happiness? Let me recommend, from my own
experience, that it be in the area of the arts—in music, in
painting, in writing, in sculpture, in dance—the range is
infinite. You will ask, is this not simply saying that one
must have a hobby? No, I do not mean a hobby. Ideally,

one should decide what one likes best to do and then train the self to earn a living in that field. But this is not always possible. Sometimes talent is insufficient for earning a living, yet enough to provide for happiness. It is then worth the effort of pursuit. You will enjoy art more if you pursue it without thought of money. Pursue it for pleasure, for release, for enrichment of the mind and spirit, for simple happiness. You will find that contentment follows. The tasks of daily life, then, are not so dreary, sorrow is lightened, loneliness becomes endurable.

Of course you must work. The will of the artist is his means of achievement, his energy. He soon learns that if he does not work, if he fills his time idly, he will be discontented and unhappy. And he is subject to all the temptations of the ordinary human being. Do I not know all too well how my own lazy will tries to deceive me?

Even after many years I can still think of a dozen ways not to sit down to my typewriter in the morning. The will needs a whip sometimes to get it started, and the mind must provide the whip. "No," mind must insist, "the flowers cannot be watered now or the newspaper read or that telephone call made, or anything else done except work."

When the will cannot escape, it performs, and when it performs, mind has to work, too. It is a curious interrelationship, this between mind and will. Mind decides for the will, and will gets to work upon mind. Long ago I learned that writing, for example, cannot depend upon the mood of the mind. Will sets mood aside and works upon mind, and mind, often reluctant at first, learns the habit of work. If mood is the ruler, then both will and mind fall into habits of lazy decay.

I know how difficult it is to understand the relationship of mind and will, especially at the beginning of learning an art. There is a certain amount of drudgery in every art. One cannot, for example, play the simplest piece of music without practice. But what joy when even the simple piece is mastered and can really be played! I recommend music, hopefully begun with a teacher, for art is most enjoyable when it is based upon accurate knowledge, even though performance never goes beyond the primary stage.

There is also sculpture, a supremely satisfying form of art, employing hands as well as mind and spirit. When my children were small and my life was overcrowded with daily duties, I found rest and release in modeling their heads in clay or plaster. I caught them on the wing as they played, and though the heads were far from perfect from a professional point of view, they were likenesses. I look at them with tender memory now that the children are grown men and women.

But why should I enumerate the arts? Art is various and always new.

What I am saying, in brief, is that the pursuit of art through some chosen form, planned for and achieved by determination and persistence, brings permanent contentment and the illumination of genuine happiness to the human spirit. Life is never dull, the creature is never bored, when he—or she—becomes the creator.

17

Courage

WHERE does it come from? Is one born with it? Is it a matter of health and strong nerves? Is it a gift that one is given or a quality that one can acquire or even a habit that one can learn by practice? How does one find courage?

What is courage?

Let me define it first by saying that it is not bravado. Bravado is the pretense of feeling what one does not feel, a show of being what one is not. Bravado may be useful sometimes, but not for long and not for any continuing effort. Bravado may give one the moment necessary for summoning the reserves of courage but one cannot depend upon it. It always breaks.

Courage does not break. It is secret strength. It is reserve power. When I hear the word *courage*, when I speak it, when I write it down, I think of a scene that took place before I was born. I know it only because my mother told me of it. She told me in the simple, unpretentious way in which she spoke of herself. How many other events she never told which might have been equal ex-

amples of courage, I do not know. This one stays with me;
I see it as though I were there. Here it is.

The place is a city deep in the interior of China, and the
time many decades ago. I do not know the exact year, but
my mother, now long dead, was then a young woman with
two small children. She was alone in the city, the only
white woman, the only white person, except the children,
for my father was away on one of his long journeys. The
season was late summer. It had been a dry, hot summer.
No rain had fallen for many weeks. The rice crop in the
fields outside the city wall had dried before harvest. The
wells in the city were low. People were hungry and
frightened. What would they have for winter food? Why
had this catastrophe fallen upon them? The gods were
angry, their priests told them. The gods were angry
because strangers, white people, were in the city.

My mother, staying close within the wall of the compound where she lived, knew what the people were
muttering outside in the streets. She was told by her
faithful servants, especially by the amah who helped her
care for the children. At their pleading she had given up
walks and shopping.

"Stay inside the gate, mistress," they begged. "Let the
people think you went away with the master."

She obeyed, but she knew that the people did not think
she had gone away. Their anger focused upon her as the
summer passed without rain and upon the house which
she had made into a home for her little family in an alien
land. Day by day she hoped for my father's return, but
she did not know when that would be. Mails were uncer-

tain, for letters were brought by foot carriers who delayed or did not arrive at all. She could only wait, hoping against hope for rain. And day after day the skies were the same blue, hard and clear. She felt the deepening despair of the people, and with it their rising fury. Sooner or later the fury would break. Over the walls, she heard the noise of parades and processions as the people carried their gods from the temples to reproach them with the sight of the bleak fields, the roads and streets deep in dust, the dried wells.

To her own God, my mother prayed, too, for rain. With all her heart she prayed as she went about her household tasks and as she cared for her children. In the hot, sleepless nights she prayed. Still there was no rain, and she knew that sooner or later the climax would come. The people would attack her and the children. In their fury, they would destroy the strangers within their city as a propitiation to the gods. It was more than her own conviction; the servants were hourly more afraid. They were faithful but they hid themselves behind the barred gate. One of them crept out at night to buy food secretly for the next day. Day and night they kept themselves quiet, speaking in low tones, hushing the children when they cried. My mother did not even play the small organ she had brought from her home in her own country, though music was always her solace.

One day dawned even more sultry than the rest. The sky was white-hot and not a breath stirred the dying leaves on the bamboos in the garden. She knew that this was the day, she told me years later. She could feel the menace that hung over the silence in the city. The streets were empty, and not even the children shouted in play.

Late that afternoon her amah came to her in terror. "Mistress," she whispered, "they are coming tonight to kill you and the children."

My mother told me that she received this news without thought of escape. She knew there was no escape. No one in the city would dare to help her or protect her. She must face whatever was to come.

At that moment, my mother said, peace came into her heart and mind. The day drew to its end and she understood what she must do. Quietly she fed the children. Then she bathed them and put on their best clothes. She dressed herself in her simple best and brushed her hair well. All this time the amah helped her but in complete amazement. What was this white woman about to do? Did she plan to kill herself and the children? Meantime the silence in the streets had broken. An ominous roar took its place. My mother knew that a mob was gathering and attack was imminent.

"Set out all our tea bowls and make fresh tea," she directed her cook. "Put the small cakes you made yesterday on plates and any fruit that we have as well."

To the gardener she said, "Open the gates of the compound—open them wide!"

They were all amazed, she told me, but she insisted and they obeyed. Then she herself opened the doors of the house and she and the children sat in the main room, they with their toys and she with her sewing. They were not frightened, for she showed no fear.

The mob howled in the streets. They surged through the open gates, carrying sticks and knives. She put down her sewing, and when they crowded the door of the house, she said, "Come in, come in and drink tea. I have been expecting you. You are welcome."

The men stared at her calm, smiling face. They took in the scene, the children playing and unafraid, the lamplit room, the tea and food on the table. My mother was pouring tea as she urged them to come in. She prattled on, telling them that her husband was not at home, that she was alone here with her good servants and the children.

They came in, uncertain and dazed, and the children, accustomed to the usually kind Chinese, left their toys and came to them without fear. My mother gave them tea, careful to hold each bowl in both hands, in courtesy to guests.

"What happened then?" I always asked this question, breathless with suspense, though I knew the story well because I wanted often to hear it.

"They drank the tea and ate the cakes," she replied. "Not at once of course, but bit by bit. They watched the children. Then everybody went away."

"Why?"

"I don't know."

"Were you afraid?"

"I was sick with fear."

"Then how did you have such courage?"

"From despair."

That is what she always said. The courage came from despair.

"If I had not had my back to the wall, if I had not had to face the situation from which there was no escape, I could not have found the courage."

Best of all, the end of the story was happy. For in the night as she lay sleepless with exhaustion, the rain fell. Unbelievable, but true! She heard it on the roof of the house and it was pure music.

"And the next morning"—she always told me by way of finish—"the whole city slept. No business was done, shops were not open. Everyone slept all day—and so did I."

I tell one more true story. This time it is about a man, a Chinese man, who saved my life when the city where I lived was attacked by a revolutionary army. It happened to be led by Communists whose slogan was to rid the country of all white people. Hence I, with my family, was caught in a place, a day, an hour, where even our Chinese friends could not save us. I will not repeat the story, for it has been told elsewhere, but let me concentrate upon this one man. He was a neighbor, the father of a family, with responsibilities. He was an intelligent man and of some education, but he made only a small salary as a teacher. He had no concern with politics, but he knew that his life would be in danger if he befriended those whom the triumphant regime opposed. Therefore he knew that if he helped white people he would probably be killed.

I shall never forget the sight of this small, dejected figure when I opened the door of the little Chinese hut where we were in hiding that day. There he stood, the picture of misery.

"I came to see that you were really here, as I heard you were," he said.

"We are here," I replied.

"I must warn you that you will be killed," he said. "Already others are killed."

My heart hardened. "Is this what you come to say?"

"No," he replied. "I say this first to make you understand your danger. You must remain here until I return. I will do my best to save you. But do not show yourselves for one instant. And do not open this door as readily as you have for me. I will knock twice and then twice again if it is I. Do not open otherwise."

We looked at each other with full understanding.

"You must think of your own family," I said.

He tried to smile and could not, and we parted with no further word. But all day I obeyed and I did not open the door again. Outside, as the dreadful hours dragged by, we heard the madness of wild human voices amid the roar of burning buildings crashing to earth. The day wore on to darkness, and still there was no sign of his return. Suddenly I heard the double knock. I opened the door enough to admit the slight frame of the Chinese. He fell to his knees and put his forehead to the earthen floor in the ancient gesture. I knew what it meant but I raised him up.

"You have done your best," I said.

"I have failed," he groaned. Then he hesitated. "I think I have failed. There is one chance—but it may fail, too. I come to ask your forgiveness, for if it fails I shall not be able to come again."

That was all. He slipped away and we waited more hours.

When he was long delayed, I had my own need of courage. I knew what would happen if he could not save us. The horrible noise of maddened mobs rose into the night. Sooner or later, and now it could not be much later, that door would burst open, that ramshackle door made of a few boards, and I would see the faces of the mob, distorted faces of fury. That would be the end of our lives. How, then, to meet it? How could I find the courage?

At this moment, I thought of my mother. Afraid, yes! In despair, yes! But out of despair had come courage. And I was in absolute despair. I had nowhere to run. There was nothing for it except to face what now seemed inevitable. When I had reached this depth, I felt a strange, cold peace fill my being. I say cold, for utter despair is cold. One can feel its chill on the skin and in the bones and in the silence of one's heart. And then for me, too, out of that cold despair rose the shape of courage. I had to have courage for there was no alternative. And I began to plan.

When that door opened, when the inevitable was about to take place, when life was to end, I must remember to put the two children in front of me so that they could be shot first. They must not be left alone. I gathered them to me, in readiness, for now I heard the footsteps, the roar growing louder and more loud, the yells and the screams of madness. The door burst open and there they were.

But in front of them all was the thin little Chinese man, very pale but calm. "You are not to be killed," he announced quietly. "You are to be taken to a certain place.

These men will escort you. I have the promise of the new commander."

And out into the night we were all marched, bayonets behind each of us, to the place designated, which indeed proved to be a place of safety, at least for the night. By the next day reinforcements arrived of our own nationals and we were taken out of the city.

Two years later when we could return again to rebuild our home, I asked the Chinese who had saved us how he had had the courage that day to risk his own life and the lives of his family.

"It was not a matter merely of saving lives, yours or mine," he replied. "It was a matter of principle. I was in despair—total despair. And so I risked everything. I threw myself against disorder and madness and mob violence. I knew I must. There was no other way. There was no other way except to face what must be faced. Then— well, I felt able to do it. I gathered our leading citizens together. We went to the commander."

In short, he accomplished the impossible. This little schoolteacher, facing a war lord, convincing him somehow that it would be unwise to allow the massacre of white people with strong nations behind them. Such courage he could not have achieved on an ordinary day. Courage, then comes of despair. Not of a small discontent, not of something that can be avoided or changed or escaped, but of something as unshakable, immovable, inescapable as death itself. Then the life force rises up, and out of despair courage is born.

It is not always a crisis that creates courage. Sometimes

it is a life deprived of joy through death or disaster. What was unshakable may still not be shaken, what was immovable still not moved, what is inescapable still not escaped. Then the despair continues as a daily source of courage— courage to live with despair and through it and around it. Of course one can choose to die. But it is a stupid choice. One denies oneself the glorious experience of facing life as it is and finding thereby the source of courage.

My concept is not new. Long ago the ancients of every country, from Greece to China, shared the symbol of the phoenix. Out of dead ashes, a golden bird soared into the sky, created none knew how, but alive. The phoenix was a sacred emblem of myth and history. It was the personal emblem of Chinese empresses. The meaning is always the same—courage out of despair, life out of death.

18

Let's Choose to Live

I T IS six o'clock in the morning—no, it is a quarter past. I have just heard the six-o'clock news. The sun rises late these autumn days, and the news is as dark as the world. But I know the sun will rise in exactly forty-three minutes. And I refuse to be a lemming. I refuse to join this increasing tide of hopeless human beings ready to yield themselves to the luxury of dying together without trying to find a way to live together.

Yes, of course it is much easier to die. A human being is divided by nature between the struggle to live and the urge to die. When enough people yield to the death longing, mass suicide is the result, and mass suicide is what we face unless we all stop being lemmings.

Oh yes, it is temptingly easy, especially at a quarter past six on a dark morning when the radio talk is only of shelters against megaton bombs. There is something very sweet in the idea of death, something temptingly easy in giving up. Death is the cessation of pain, an end to loneliness, a refuge from cruel and unloving persons. Who does not dream of death in the darkness before dawn? It is

all but impossible to believe in the dawn. Our novelists
and playwrights are enamored of death, and shrewd merchants sell their gloom to a helpless public. The horrors of
nuclear war are apparently to be assuaged by other sav-
age animality and decadent violence. Thus we drag each
other down deeply and more deeply into the death side of
our natures. The beatnik, unshaven, unwashed, parading
his hopelessness, is the symbol of our temptation. It takes
an effort of will not to be a beatnik. Lemmings are
beatniks and beatniks are lemmings. I refuse to be either.
I was not born to be a lemming or trained to be one, and
beatniks smell.

I remember my intrepid mother in the days when I was
so small that I had to stretch my mind to understand why
in the blackness of a winter night she disguised herself in
ragged Chinese garments, stained her face brown, and
with a small canvas bag of silver dollars, slipped through
our compound gate into the surrounding Chinese city.
She had dark hair and eyes and could pass for a Chinese,
and my father could not go with her because he was tall
and fair and had eyes of sterling blue and would have
been mobbed because all foreigners were supposed to be
rich. In the dead of the night, the intrepid American
woman crept among the mat huts of famine refugees
encamped on the city wall and into each she put a dollar.
No, it did not end the famine or prevent another, but
what she did was on the side of life. She kept families and
human beings alive until something better could be devised. She was always on the side of life, and I am her
daughter. I was born to live and I choose life.

I am not limiting my definition of life to mere survival. For me, the question of building a shelter against nuclear attack is academic and I waste no time thinking about it. Obviously it is impossible for everyone to be sheltered in time of nuclear war, and I am convinced from past experience with wars that however fine a shelter I made for myself and my family, it would be impossible for me not to open the door to let others in.

I remember a war in the city of Nanking when my house was full of frightened people, the floors heaving with the people in the basement, and every inch of floor space above crowded with human beings. The stairs were especially valuable as sitting space. Most of the people were strangers to me but common danger made us one family. It could all happen again, but this time we are told we cannot open the door of a shelter. Well, I open doors, and that is all there is to it, and so I have to think of ways toward peace other than nuclear war, because peace is necessary if we are to live.

So why not begin by making a fresh start toward the Russians? And the Chinese? I don't mean those endless meetings in Warsaw with the representative from the Communist Government in Peking. Such meetings are only detrimental, for they deceive us into thinking we are doing something when we are not. I mean a rational and realistic approach based upon true knowledge of the nature of the peoples who do not understand us and whom we do not understand.

Let's begin by making sure that we mean the same things by the same words. For example, yesterday I visited the home of a friend who recently adopted a little half-American orphan from Japan. His first grade teacher had given the child an intelligence test the day before, and the result had been lower than the parents expected.

"He says such odd things," the father explained sadly.

"What sort of thing?" I inquired.

"Well, she asked him how many legs a dog has. He said two! Now he knows a dog has four legs, and when I asked him why he said two, he replied that it depended upon what legs the teacher meant. That makes no sense, does it?"

"It makes good sense," I told him. "In Japan, the front two legs of a cat or a squirrel or a dog are called hands, not legs. From his point of view, based on his experience, so different from yours, he was right."

The eyes of the parents opened and the little boy's IQ went up at once, as I could see.

Much of the trouble in the world today comes from a simple misunderstanding of words and terms and meanings, especially when we have no common language. Another misunderstanding, and the deepest of all, is of values. What one people may value most is not always valued as highly by others, but do we know it? Or why it is so? Or what to do about it? Or do we know that we don't need to kill each other because we differ? Military forces are useful only as police are useful in a community. I can conceive that in an enlightened community of the future even police may not be necessary. Misunderstanding and disagreement are merely deepened and solidified by show of force. Everyone knows that we have force and that our enemies have force, and yet the situation grows no better.

Yet we also have informed people, trained in the use of human understandings—not as many as we need, but we have them. Other countries have them, in Europe and Asia, South America and Africa. They are scattered but they exist. It is time to give these persons a chance through a period of trust and trial. It is the only rational opportunity left to us at this hour, the right-about-face toward life that they could give us instead of our steady, downward march toward death, a march as stupid, I insist, as that of lemmings hurrying senselessly to drown themselves in the sea.

Who knows? A miracle could happen, as miracles have happened before. And what is a miracle? Nothing more than the utilization of hitherto unused forces—in this case the forces of great and good human beings, those who believe in life, those whose motives are pure, those who *live,* but not for themselves alone.

19

Our Sexual Revolution

I HAVE NOW lived almost as long in my own country as I lived in Asia, but not quite. I must live another decade in my house in this American landscape before I can say that half my life has been spent in my own country. Yet these years have been enough to reveal many changes in my American people. Reflecting, I conclude that no other in the world has changed as much as we Americans have changed since the end of World War II, with the exception of Communist China. We have grown in many ways, although it is too soon to tell whether the change is for the better or worse. Our new awareness of the world of nations and people, our amazing readiness to adapt as we come to know these other cultures, have shaken our culture to its foundations. Perhaps this signifies an outer shell to our own culture which has long been representing inner expansion and the impulse for change.

Nowhere is this more apparent than in our new ethics of sex. The change is so abrupt, so far-reaching, that we are all dazed by it. Nor can we comfort ourselves by

saying that it is only the young who are changed. The
new sex standards are to be found among men and women
of any age, but especially among women. Even older
women are allowing themselves a sexual freedom that
would have horrified not only their mothers but themselves in the prewar period. They are still horrified
enough to keep their secrets to themselves, and yet, half
laughing, half shamefaced, they will confess to some
woman friend that they are having extramarital affairs.
Among unmarried women there is little shame, but still
not much talk.

I confess to my own sense of shock when a friend, an
older, unmarried woman apparently of the highest re-
spectability and with considerable public responsibility,
told me tranquilly that she had only a few years before
carried on a two-year affair with an equally respectable
but married man. She explained, with no sense of guilt,
that she wanted to know what sexual experience was
before she grew too old.

"Did you love the man?" I asked.

"No, but I liked him enough," she replied with calm.

"And why did you stop the affair?" I asked.

"His job was moved to another city and it was too
inconvenient for us to meet," she said.

"Have you ever regretted it?" I asked.

"Not at all," she said. "I am very grateful to him and I
think he is to me."

"But he was married," I argued. "Had you no concern
for his wife?"

"He needed something more, and I supplied that need,"

she said. "I doubt he's had another affair. I rather imagine he's gone back to his wife and is quite contented. Indeed, he never left her, nor does she know, I am sure, because she was my friend, too—still is. We often have luncheon together."

"And she really does not know?"

"Does not and never will."

And what about my handsome, fifty-five-year-old friend, a divorcée who, contemplating remarriage with a man of her own age, felt that she could not proceed unless she knew what he would be as a sexual partner? He was satisfactory, but later she decided against him because they were unequal intellectually and perhaps socially. The commonsense with which she came to this conclusion denied any feelings of guilt or loss of self-respect, and can only prove my point that our sex standards have changed, especially for women.

And yet in one way I do not think the change in women is any greater than that in men, for men accept the change in women with surprising equanimity and even with pleasure. A generation ago they demanded chastity in their wives and virginity in their brides. Now half of the young women who marry, if I am to trust statistics, already are not virgins. It does not seem to matter to most men whether they marry virgins or not. This can only mean a real equalization of sex standards, since women, always realistic where men are concerned, have neither required nor expected their husbands to be virgins at marriage. It was hoped that husbands would remain faithful after marriage, but women have always distrusted

other women and have been watchful on this score and
ready to forgive the man at least once if the worst, though
expected and feared, did happen.

All this amounts to what is being called—and quite
properly, I think—a sexual revolution. There are several
causes for this revolution. The effects of two world wars
have changed both men and women. Men living for long
periods abroad in the atmosphere of imminent death and
away from home ties and restraints seem no longer to
demand chastity in women. Instead, they encourage sexual freedom, partly because they have grown accustomed
to women who have abandoned, or who never had, the
old standards of sexual morality. And such women are
sexually attractive to men. They can find swift satisfaction
without the delays of courtship. This attitude has been
communicated to American women at home. Whatever
man finds attractive, woman will try to become—at least
physically.

A second cause for the sexual revolution is in the
commercialization of sex. Commercial minds are quick to
discover what influences the mind and heart of woman. It
is man. Hence the many devices to sell sex. Even laundry
soap and shoe polish have their part in the sex dance. To
the greedy and artful commercial mind, everything can be
shaped and compelled into the sex pattern and so bring in
dollars. Yet we Americans are not more interested in sex
than other peoples are, or are we more sexual physically
than others are. That we appear to be so in the eyes of the
world is only because American men and women are
searching for new ways of understanding each other and

reaching real companionship and communication. The old, practical relationship of pioneer days is ended. Woman is no longer an indispensable part of the household ménage or the Western frontier. A man can get good meals in a restaurant or hotel, he can even make a comfortable home for himself in his own house or apartment. The same is true for a woman. Neither is essential to the other in practical terms now in our modern world. What remains, nevertheless, is the natural and undying desire for sex companionship on varying levels.

For some, this level is only physical. For others, perhaps particularly for women, whose sexual nature is not so focal or so simple as man's, it includes the wish for a home and children. At the highest levels, it includes mental and spiritual understanding, as well as physical and familiar. The eternal truth is that men and women are happiest when they find their complement in each other. In the old days when life and safety depended on such partnership, it was easier to find happiness together than it is today. But the need is as great, perhaps even greater, since the old opportunities no longer exist.

Today the complementarity between men and women has to be discovered in personality, in tastes, in ideals and ambitions. This is not to ignore the primary and primal function of physical sex, for this aspect of sex pervades all other communication. The difference in its use is whether the first approach to complete companionship is physical or whether the physical is the final consummation.

At present, in our searching for each other, man and woman, the physical is frequently the first approach because it is the easiest. If it only precedes the delight of mind meeting mind and heart reaching heart, it performs a function. Too often, however, absorption in the physical prevents further communication and consequent mutual understanding. Love is essential for such development and love is not contained in lust. I believe, therefore, that love, leading to understanding, is essential to physical sex if the latter is to be complete in its expression and consequent enjoyment. This is true at least for sophisticated and intelligent men and women.

Whether this complete expression and total enjoyment is best developed by marriage is becoming a question— not a new one, however. It has been a question for many centuries in many countries. The answer is not relevant here except as it affects the birth of children. Fortunately or unfortunately, there are as yet no means of prevention perfect enough, short of sterility, to guarantee that no child will result from the physical union of a man and a woman. Technical means do not serve in moments of emotion and unexpected impulse or even of laziness and carelessness. Certainly in this era of changing attitudes and shifting standards, no amount of frank warning and availability of birth control implements has served to prevent the birth of 250,000 children who have no families and are, in fact, born displaced persons here in our own country.

I am setting down these thoughts after a visit to a great city hospital. One part of it houses children although they are not physically ill. They were born there in the hospital and were never taken away because no one wants them. It is these children whom I went to see—hundreds of them. I walked between the cribs. The children lie in strange silence, listening. To what? I listened, too. I heard a mechanical heart, a machine in the wall. Its beat simulates the beat of a mother's heart before her child is born. The sound keeps the children quiet. They remain unborn.

How is this possible? It simply is, for it is a fact. It is a tragic aspect of our sexual revolution. Let me reflect for a moment upon this unwanted child's part in the revolution. A child when he is born is already a human being, and as such he has a right to the opportunities and the joys of life. He should not be burdened with the cruel circumstances of his birth, over which he has no control. There is no such person as an illegitimate child, and this has often been truly said. He appears according to the laws of nature. What is illegitimate is the condemning environment into which he is born. Innocent though he is, he is born guilty of a crime he has not committed. He suffers for it all his life. Even though he learns through maturity to accept what he is and to accommodate himself to the facts, yet in his secret heart is the eternal *why* of his birth. Why did those two persons, his natural father and mother, create his being? Why, having done so, did they reject him? Above all, why did his mother give him away? However much one explains the agony of the giving, however one mouths the usual phrases—"She had no home for you." . . . "She thought it would be better for you to have a real home and parents who could love you and take care of you"—the secret heart believes that she could have thought of some way if she had wanted to do so. Yet the truth is that in our present society there is no way for the unwed mother to keep her child, for if she keeps him the burden still falls on the child. "Who is your father?" The question in itself is cruel accusation. The unhappy mother may concoct a fantasy of death but she cannot maintain it. Sooner or later the wise child discovers the fraud. Then the old demand returns: "Why did they let me be born?"

The answer, if the unwed mother is honest, is that she could not help it. She tries in every way she knows to prevent the birth. If possible, there is a marriage. But sometimes she is mature enough, however few her years, to know that there should not be marriage. She realizes that she has entered into a physical relationship that can never grow into other areas of mind and spirit. Such a marriage is no foundation for a home and she refuses it. Sometimes she accepts it at any cost, and with it a permanent unhappiness which cannot provide the child with the atmosphere he needs for full development, but which at least spares him the accusation of being illegitimate. Sometimes she tries to stop the child's being born. She tries abortion.

Abortion has been called "one of the great epidemic diseases of our time." Of all the natural deaths in New York City in 1962, more than half were from criminal abortion. It is said that there are more than 1,200,000 abortions or attempted abortions in the United States every year. That is, to every four births there is an abortion. One hospital in New York City reports six or seven abortions a day. We may expect a rising number, for pre-Castro Cuba is no longer a refuge for women who went there for abortions. Since abortion is illegal in the United States except for medical reasons, women here now resort to criminal abortion, at the risk of their lives. The woman who seeks such abortion is not always unwed. She may be married and not wish to have the child or, increasingly likely in these days of sexual revolution, the child's father may not be her husband. Her child then will be as illegitimate as though she were unwed.

How can there be sexual freedom between man and woman without producing the homeless, unwanted child? What is the answer? Various nations have tried to find it. Asia segregated male and female at an early age and maintained a strict guard over the female. But modern ways are influencing even ancient Asia, and it is only a question of time and rising industrial life before it will face the same problems that we in the West face. Young women in India and Japan are flocking into offices and factories where they work side by side with young men. Japan is trying legalized abortions and is managing at least to keep her population stable. Yet legalized abortions, even there, are not enough to cope with the unwelcome child, and illegal abortions continue in ever increasing numbers. Sweden tries to solve the problem by recognizing the unwed mother and her child as respectable citizens, but if this is done on a wide scale, we shall see a return to matriarchy, the home and the family where man is not essential except as a stud animal. This I consider a real threat to our society. The highest civilizations—the longest to last and I believe the most successful in human terms—are those which have come the closest to achieving real understanding and mutual appreciation between men and women.

The American family at its best is a unit unsurpassed, in my observation. The problem today is how to maintain it at its best when the new sexual freedom allows women to be promiscuous. For whether a woman has one affair or twenty, it is the same promiscuity. She has shown herself available.

"It is a strain for a man to live in these modern times," an attractive middle-aged man confessed to me once. "There are so many available women nowadays."

"Married or single?" I inquired.

"It makes no difference," he said. "They are equally available."

We talked for a while of what it means to a society when its women make themselves "available." We agreed that it was a sign of the breakdown of the family as we know it. For our family system is expressed in patriarchal terms. Man's nature is such that he remains within the family system only when he is the head of the family and responsible for its maintenance and existence and thus is essential. If he absents himself, if he is irresponsible, if he is promiscuous, the family, and with it society, drifts into a matriarchy because the woman is thereby compelled to assume full responsibility.

Industrialization tends to compel this drift for, with the present high cost of living, an increasing number of women are leaving the home to work outside. This in itself removes part of the responsibility for the family from men, and if the woman earns more than the man, may entirely absolve him from responsibility. So profound, so complex and yet so tenuous, is the relationship between man and woman that the two will certainly draw apart unless they are united by more than physical bonds, or even by their parental duties.

A man's relation with his own child, if his position is minimized, dissolves rather easily. I have observed this in divorced couples. There is often a passionate determination on the part of the father, at first, to keep his hold on his children. The law is against him, of course, for it recognizes the mother's claim as supreme unless she is proven unfit. At any rate, it is not long before the father, in his new freedom, begins to see his children less and less often until at last they all but cease to see him and he knows but ignores or forgets.

Observing, I sometimes wonder if, after all, the family is an artificial unit, a relic of the days when man was the hunter of food, the hewer of wood and the drawer of water for the woman and child. Yet I know it is not so. I know that the only completely happy life for man and for woman is their life, first together, and then with their children. I am a firm believer that no marriage can be really happy, and no home a happy one for the children as well, unless man puts woman first and woman puts man first, each for the other the giver of every good gift. Children are the fruit of this total love, but children are not to take first place in the woman's heart. That belongs to the man. When woman allows the helplessness of a child to creep into that center sacred to man, it is an usurpation, and home and the family are undermined.

All this is preliminary for solution. We shall not see a change in our society until we see a change in our education. Women should be educated for men, and men should be educated for women, for in the other and with the other, each finds his and her own fullest development. At present we have no such education. Yes, I know that we teach sex education in many of our schools, but sex education as it is now taught is not what I mean. I said education of men and women for each other, and physical sex is only a part of the whole, and perhaps a lesser part.

I do not forget the day that a certain young daughter of mine came home from school and threw her books on the table and burst into tears.

Upon my solicitous inquiry she made reply: "I do wish they wouldn't keep trying to teach sex at school," she sobbed. "It takes all the romance out of love."

What they should have been teaching was love between the sexes. And what is that love? It is more than the mating instinct, it is more than physical sex, but it includes both. It is the most complete relationship in human life, and merely to teach the physical and technical does indeed rob love of its heart and soul.

True education for life begins, I believe, in the recognition that men and women are totally different from each other. Even in their common humanity they are different.

They look at the same scenes and see them differently. When both are artists dealing with the same human stuff as their material, they create differently. In this is the value of sex. What man and woman become as a result of their difference, what they create out of the combination of their differences in complementing, creates wholeness. Without combination and complementing, creation is warped and one-sided whether that creation be music, painting, writing, politics and national life—or a child.

For when I say creation, I mean the word in a world sense, beginning in the home and including every phase of life in the universe. A woman can and should, if she has the confidence of man, move into every area of human existence and still remain a woman. Indeed, she loses her value if she becomes less. We hear the complaint these days that women are becoming masculine and men are becoming feminine—that is to say unmasculine, weak, etc. I am amused when I hear this complaint. Is woman indeed so powerful in her nature that she compels men to become weak? If so, is not man then inherently weak? Such questions are idle for the complaint is idle.

If woman must be kept segregated and subdued, a sex symbol instead of a whole woman, in order that man may maintain his strength and his position, then he is indeed the inferior. But I do not believe that either sex is inferior to the other. Each has its individuality and each is necessary to the other in every aspect of life. We need to know what the individuality is, however, in order to instruct our young in the functions of sex in its totality. And they must be taught to realize that the totality is never achieved, with its maximum of sexual enjoyment, unless knowledge is complete.

I do not believe, therefore, in the segregation of the sexes as Asia practiced it. On the contrary, I believe in nonsegregation at all levels from birth to death. Men and women should face life together, solving its problems with confidence that solutions can be found in their combined knowledge, judgment and energy, and enjoy its solutions the more because they work together for solution and enjoyment. This man and woman can do only when they freely allow each to be himself, herself, without strictures and division of duties. There are some women who are better ditch-diggers than some men. Therefore let them be ditch-diggers. Some men are better housekeepers than women. Therefore let them be housekeepers. But allow the woman to dig the ditch in her own way, and the man to keep the house in his own way. This they must, out of the difference in their natures.

What needs to be done now is to explore those two differing but complementary natures, these two attitudes upon life which, combined, make the total view. Alas, we have no such literature to help us in our society. Of books on sex there are a plethora, but they deal primarily with physical sex whereas the truth is that we cannot understand or even experience physical sex fully until it takes its place in the whole relationship that knits man and woman into one being. Woman must be wooed, these books suggest, in order that she will respond satisfactorily to man in the act of physical sex. Yet if this be the only purpose of the wooing, she will still not respond except

superficially. She will respond to man's full content only
when the physical act comes as the expression of a complete life with him in all areas.

Nor is it always the man who must woo. Woman, in
love with man, is quite capable of using her body to
attract him, and indeed she is so taught to do in the
shallows of our modern civilization. He may yield, but it
will not be to her content, for man, too, does not live by
flesh alone. He discards woman after he discovers that
there is no more to her than flesh and bone and a hank of
hair.

This I believe is what we must teach our young male
and female. With full knowledge of each other, with
respect for the individual and the desire for each to
develop to full capacity—neither shaping nor being
shaped—man and woman learn to live in cooperation. For
the nature of man and of woman is manifold in function.

I stood in recent months in the entrance to the Ele-
phanta Caves near Bombay, India. Long ago the caves
were made into a vast temple. There, facing me as I
entered, was a monumental image of Deity. It is a great
head with three faces, so huge that it towered above me
into the lofty ceiling. I examined these faces. The central
one was the strongest and the most beautiful, a calm face,
transcendent in dignity. The other two faces were in
profile, one gentle and feminine, the other lean and cruel.

"Why are there three faces to Deity?" I inquired of an
Indian friend.

"Because Deity, like the human being, has more than
one aspect," he replied. "The central face is the face of the

Creator. The gentle face is the feminine quality of the Creator's being. The cruel face is his destructive aspect."

"Must there be the feminine?" I asked.

"Assuredly. For Deity has also the preserving, guarding function, which is feminine."

"And must Deity destroy?" I asked again.

"He must destroy if he continues to create, for these are the two opposites in his nature."

The deities of the ancient world are always modeled after the human creature, for Asia understands human nature better than we do. And Asia's deities are always manifold in one, as human beings are. To understand that manifold is to understand ourselves who were from the beginning created male and female. Together we create, we preserve, two in one and one in two. In us, also, is the destructive element, the desire even to destroy each other as we daily do when we fail to love completely.

Where does such knowledge begin, so that our young may be educated? It begins in the home, in the treatment the husband and wife, mother and father, accord each to the other. The boy child, in his desire to emulate his father, soon absorbs from him the attitudes of domination over, or consideration for, the wife and mother. What he learns at home he will practice in the community. So, too, the girl child will learn from her parents. If her mother is rebelliously subordinate or contemptuously superior to the husband and father, the girl will never understand her own capacity for love or those of the man she will one day marry.

For our young enter into marriage almost totally ignorant of each other. They are instructed incorrectly, or at best inadequately, even in physical sex, and of anything more they hardly dream. Ah, there it is—they do not dream nowadays! They voice their deep discontent in their popular songs, universally sad and lacking in sexual relation. Out of this hunger and discontent, they seize upon physical sex almost with desperation.

A handsome youth put it thus in my presence a few days ago. He was speaking of women whom he knew. "Men seem unable these days to find any common ground with women—except the brief satisfaction of biological need. And that's not enough. It leaves us cold."

"That is the way women feel, too," I said. "They think you want nothing more from them, and so that's all they give."

As a result of this sort of desperation, there are born each year a quarter of a million unwanted children. For the wanted child is the child born of love and not of desperation. Am I suggesting that we must teach our youths romantic love? Perhaps I am, but for romanticism let me substitute idealism. At least I suggest that we teach respect for human beings, above all for human beings as male and female.

It is not to be expected that every time the male and female come together in the unison of physical sex a child will or should be conceived. Nevertheless, it is true that with each such act a child may be conceived. It is that child who must receive respect, that possible child. Since as yet there has not been devised a sure preventive for such conception, short of surgery, and though such a preventive will assuredly be found someday, it will not always be used when it should be used unless the man and woman have first learned the necessary control over their emotions. Wherein lies the secret of control? It lies in the discipline of the mind over the body, and the instrument of the mind is the will. The mind must be informed by knowledge and by idealism in order to strengthen the will.

I suggest, therefore, that our education of the young, contained in knowledge and idealism, should include respect for the unborn child, the possible child. The gravest responsibility in life is to bring a child into this world. Under the best of conditions it is a responsibility, for it is an arbitrary act. None of us has asked to be born. Two other persons decided upon that. Where society welcomes the child, his chances for life are good. Where society does not welcome the child, where he is not wanted, not expected—worst of all, where there is no family to receive him, where even his mother considers him a disaster, and his father does not recognize him, where his very existence is a sorrowful secret—then indeed he is to be pitied. He will never receive the respect and love due him, unless he finds a substitute family through adoption. More than half the time, however, he will not find that family and he must struggle against the disadvantages of growing up among strangers and alone. For if he does not find father and mother, sisters and brothers, he is alone and among strangers. The primary environment cannot be replaced by employees in a hospital or an orphanage or by paid foster parents.

Yet he enters life bravely. Every boy and girl should learn how bravely a baby enters life. It is no slight ordeal, this matter of birth. None of us understands exactly how the transition is made from the warm, liquid world of prenatal life into the totally different atmosphere. Floating in that gentle sea, the baby need not exert his lungs to breathe, or does he fear a blow or know a touch or suffer hunger. He is altogether protected by his mother. Then comes the moment of birth. Can he survive it? It is the moment of gravest danger for him—more dangerous, perhaps, than he will ever meet again until his death. Will he live? He has only a few seconds, at most a few minutes, in which to decide. As Hippocrates once said, "The occasion is instant." Within the brief space of time his lungs, which he has never used, must begin to function. Until now his mother has supplied him with oxygen, and the placental system has disposed, too, of the carbon dioxide in his blood. Now he must do everything for himself. To make it more difficult, his lungs are not clear. They contain fluid, perhaps drawn in before he was born or perhaps created by himself—we do not know. Yet he has to inflate his lungs, expel the fluid and draw in air, or he will die. And all this must be done, I repeat, in seconds or at best in a very few minutes. Meanwhile he is in a surprising new environment. The comforting darkness he has known until now is gone, and he is surrounded by sharp light. Instead of the warm, soft liquid he has hitherto felt on his tender skin, he now feels hard objects of some sort. He is chilled, too, by the new atmosphere. He even feels his own body heavy, which until now has been weightless. Through all this he has only instinct and impulse to guide him.

A weak child cannot cope with the situation. He never draws the first breath which catapults him into the new world. He yields and dies. But he is in the minority. The life force is strong, and 99 percent of the babies born do fight for their lives. They struggle to draw the first breath which alone will accommodate them to the new environment, sudden and unexpected, in which they find themselves. It is an act of instinctive courage and it deserves our respect. Therefore, I would, if I were the teacher, educate the young male and female first of all in what it means to be born, to struggle for life, and then to find oneself deprived of family and home. Perhaps when this lonely individual becomes a reality for them, they will consider their own bodies, their sexual capacities and functions, and perceive the necessity to understand and to control and to use wisely the strong and significant power of sex.

Am I implying the word *sacred?* It is not a fashionable word or one often used in our modern times. It is tarnished by its connection with puritanical religion. Nevertheless, I will use it, for I believe that the physical creation is sacred, as art is sacred, and for the same reason. It is creation. And until we imbue our young male and female with recognition of this as a fact, we shall see them desecrate their functions until the sexual act becomes no more than an elimination.

I am not advocating less sex. I am advocating more and better sex, sex that does not shame and degrade an innocent child, sex that brings joy and ecstasy and triumphant pride and, above all, reverence for life.

20

Wanted: A New Morality

TWO LADIES sit in my drawing room, waiting for me.
We have an appointment to discuss a coming event.
It is to be a benefit for the work to which I am presently
devoting myself, a foundation established under my name
for the welfare and education of children of American
servicemen and Asian women. These children are now in
the seven countries of Asia where our men are stationed
and, knowing these countries as I do, I am saddened by
the plight of little half-American children born out of wedlock in countries where there is no provision for such children. Their plight is worsened by the fact that in Asia
children belong to the father, not the mother, and without
fathers they are not registered at birth and so have no
opportunity for education and jobs. They are stateless.

My mind is occupied with these children as I enter the
room, these half-American children, the result of careless
encounter, and growing up anyhow in the lowest echelons
of Asian society. What can be done to help them or, better
still, to prevent their birth? I am not prepared for the first
remark made by one of the ladies.

"We were just discussing The Pill," she says brightly.

The Pill needs no explanation here. Everyone, at least in the United States, knows what The Pill is. It is a small object, not to be compared to the nuclear bomb in size, but its potential effect upon our society may be even more devastating.

I sit down before I reply. "I fear The Pill is not practical in Asian countries," I tell the ladies. "It is cheap here in relation to our average income, but three dollars and a half a month is about a fourth of a family's income in Asia. That is still too much for an Asian girl to pay, and I doubt that our men . . . well, it would not be practical, either, for them to provide The Pill for the girls they consort with . . . too many of their encounters are casual and. . . ."

The ladies exchange looks. Now they laugh.

"We aren't thinking of the girls abroad. We are thinking of our own daughters," the elder one says.

I know those daughters. They are charming girls in their late teens, well-educated, pretty and smartly dressed.

"Surely you don't mean that Pat and Sue would—"

"We don't know," the younger lady says frankly.

"We just don't know," the older lady agrees. "And I'd rather give my Sue The Pill than run the risk of an illegitimate child or an abortion."

"Times have changed," the younger one chimes in.

We spend an hour in agitated, intense talk, I the listener. The problem is real to these American mothers, facing as parents the same situation that our servicemen are creating abroad, the change in our sex standards—a change made abrupt by the arrival of The Pill. Yes, The Pill is a social bomb both for America and Asia. Never before has Asia faced in such numbers the presence of young Western men accustomed at home to girls who use The Pill and thereby remove from men the necessity of sex control.

Yes, of course Asia has dealt firmly with the facts of life, and for centuries. She separated male from female very early. A boy, at seven, went to the men's quarters and lived with his own kind. To provide against the sex urges of adolescence, marriages were early and arranged. To allow for a man's fancies after marriage, he could bring into his house as concubine any woman who attracted him, and her child bore his name and belonged to his family. There was no such person in Asia as the illegitimate child—not until now. Today there are thousands, nearly all of them half American. Our men have taken our problem to Asia.

As for The Pill, I am no stranger to it, I with my seven daughters married and unmarried. My youngest three are still in their teens.

. . . At this point, it occurs to me to ask their advice as I write. I have heard mothers, now let me hear daughters. I summon them and they sit here in my workroom at this very moment, the two who are at home this morning, aged sixteen and seventeen.

"What do your friends do about The Pill?" I ask. "For that matter, what do you do?"

They are frank, as usual. We are a frank family. I have no secrets from my daughters and they know it. I cannot be bothered with secrets, I tell them. It would be too much trouble to hide my own tracks.

The elder of the two, the cheerful, gay, outgoing one, the sometimes naughty seventeen-year-old one, answers promptly as usual. "Well, in the first place, girls can get The Pill easily enough. They do get it and many of them use it."

"They think it is all right to use it?" I ask.

"If a girl loves a boy, or even likes him, she thinks it is all right," she replies.

"And you?"

"I haven't liked any boy that much yet. I don't know what I'd do if I did. Maybe I'd still want to marry him first. Yes, I'd rather do that."

"Why?"

She hesitates long enough for the younger one, my quiet, thoughtful one, to speak for herself.

"I think it depends on the individual girl. I don't think I'd want to use The Pill. I'd feel that I was somehow interfering with a life—someone's life."

"You wouldn't think just of yourself—or the boy?"

"No."

I can understand. She herself is the daughter of an American serviceman. Her birth mother is Japanese. She is my dear adopted daughter. My four youngest adopted daughters are all the children of American servicemen and Asian mothers. They are deeply conscious of the right of a child to be born into a good home, with both father and mother waiting for them. The Pill does not tempt them. They know what they want. They want first of all to be persons in their own right. If marriage comes, they want it to be stable and enduring, a shelter and a place of growth for their children.

"But what of other girls, those without your experience of life?" I ask.

They interchange looks. "Most girls think it is all right to use The Pill."

"Especially the girls in the city. Here in the country, not so many."

These were their answers. Of course there is nothing new in this for me, either. I live among the young and hear their constant talk, always centering about sex.

"Much more important," I say, "is whether you think it is right or wrong for girls to use The Pill. That is what I want to know."

"We don't know what is right and wrong except for ourselves," the gay child says.

The other one nods. "We are different from the other girls," she says.

It is as far as they will or perhaps can go. They have decided what sort of persons they wish to be and beyond that, as yet, they have no answers.

They left me alone again with my own thoughts.

The Pill, of course, is designed to make sex intercourse "safe" whenever it takes place, either before or after marriage, and "safe" in this case means prevention of pregnancy.

For me, the greatest argument against sex intercourse before marriage has always been the possible child. As yet The Pill, in spite of all the talk, is still not solving the problem of the child born out of wedlock, even here in our own country. Statistics now give the figure of 250,000 children born out of wedlock each year in the United States, over half of them from high school girls whose mothers did not provide them with The Pill. Of these children less than half find adoptive homes. The rest grow up as best they can in orphanages, foster homes and baby hospitals. They still bear, as long as they live, the stigma of the illegitimate child. Modern as we are with The Pill, we have made no change by law to improve the status of the child born out of wedlock. The father of the child assumes no responsibility. The mother assumes very little. She bears the child and turns it over to an adoption agency or to some other agency. The child bears the whole brunt of its birth into life.

Am I indignant? Yes, I am! Of all the hateful injustices that I see here in my dearly loved country, this is the injustice I hate the most. It is cruelty to a child at its very conception, cruelty to compel it to life against its own knowledge, cruelty to let it be born and then to give it away to strangers, cruelty to deprive it of its right to love and a welcoming family. It is the cruelty of total irresponsibility. It is the irresponsibility that I resent. No one should bring a child into the world without responsibility for the act, or risk the act without responsibility.

Now, however, The Pill is here. It is possible that if all girls use it steadily, the illegitimate child need not be born. As soon as a girl matures, she may, if she wishes, begin to take The Pill. She is then free from the risk of a possible child. But is she free of responsibility? It is ironic that all these birth control implements are for the woman, not for the man. The few that have been provided for him he prefers not to use, for one excuse or another. His only concern seems to remain wholly free of control, and in order to remove the possibility of fathering a child, he concentrates his efforts upon discovering implements for the woman which will provide no trouble for him.

Yet even The Pill is not a perfect implement for the woman. No one knows what the long range effects of The Pill will be. There are women for whom it is dangerous, and if not immediately dangerous, still attended by discomfort. Nausea afflicts many women when they take The Pill, and circulatory discomforts attack others. Implements are not pleasant or entirely practical for the woman, either. The old-fashioned diaphragm is always unpleasant to attach and tend. The new coil is fraught with possible dangers. No human organ can exist beyond the possibility of disease if a foreign object remains permanently imbedded in it, certainly not as delicate an organ as the uterus.

It seems that nature itself is determined to connect the sexual act, for woman, with the creation of a child. An operation which renders a woman permanently sterile is a serious operation, although the operation for a man is a slight one, its only grave effect the fact that he is thereby rendered permanently sterile. Yet, if he is so willing not to have a child by a woman, why is he not willing to be sterilized? Then he can indulge himself as much as he pleases, to his own demoralization, but at least not to the criminal extent of producing a child without a home into which to be born. Perhaps it is time for women to require that men be sterilized before promiscuity. If the sex act is to be nothing more than fun or release or an indoor sport for a man, then let us sterilize him and enjoy him—and be enjoyed by him—without risk of damage from implements or risk of a child.

It is a pitiful thing to hear a young girl say, when she is pregnant: "No, I am not married to him but I love him. I love him so much that I want to give him everything."

"But you had no right to give him a child," I tell her. "And he had no right to allow you to give him what he does not want—this helpless little child!"

The new freedom, therefore, consequent upon The Pill, which accepts the sex act as merely an act of love or liking or simply "fun," should require by law that a man give proof of sterility before he approaches a girl sexually without marriage. If she is the one to make the approach, then she should demand proof of sterility or realize that she is taking a risk. If a man is not sterile, if by mischance she has a child, she and the man should be held equally and totally responsible for the child's welfare and education.

But what is the sex act when it is nothing but release or sport? It is nothing—it is less than nothing. It becomes tiresome and even disgusting. It loses all meaning as time goes on. Consider the prostitute in any country where she is to be found. She goes through her dreary round night after night. At least for her it is a livelihood, but how wretched and stupid a way to earn one's bread, how joyless and how mean! It is in very truth a dog's life.

Consider also the promiscuous man and woman. They move from one bed to another, yet all beds are only beds, unless love attends—not casual love but faithful, mutual love, deeply rooted in all of life. The sex act is the most intimate communication possible between two human beings, the one man, the other woman. When it is carelessly and casually bestowed, the degradation is profound. I have not seen a promiscuous man or woman who did not show the open effects of this degradation. His–her spiritual quality is gone; he–she is animal, this human being created after some divine image whose beginning we still do not know!

The chief commandment of the new morality, therefore, is that this closest and most intimate relationship between man and woman is not to be misused as mere physical relaxation or sport. For if it is so misused, the effects are harmful to the personality. There is a loss.

Let me resume my thoughts. It must be true that marriage, if entered into with due consideration and with deep love, is still the most fulfilling and rewarding of human relationships. It must be true or marriage would not be the most widely maintained relationship everywhere in the world. The happiest and most meaningful moments in marriage are those that are the most intimate. But if these most intimate acts have already been used elsewhere and have lost their meaning as profound communication, then even the marriage is robbed of its full meaning.

. . . At this point I pause. The door opens and my young married daughter comes in to see how I fare on this stormy day. We have fine storms on our side of the mountain, and while I write the roar of crashing clouds has been echoing through the valley which my window overlooks.

It occurs to me now to read my thoughts aloud to this capable and downright young woman, the mother of five children of her own and of several others whom she somehow gathers into her house. The latter are the children of working mothers, and she cherishes them in a mood of fire and indignation. She is that most modern of young mothers, for she believes that mothers belong at home with their children. Among other occupations she is also the confidante of my teenage daughters.

"Read me what you are writing," she commands.

Obedient parent that I am, I comply. She listens, intent on every word. Her mind is keen and incisive. She is not afraid to praise or criticize.

When I finish she speaks: "You haven't written down the real reason why The Pill is given to young girls nowadays."

I am properly humble. "What is the real reason, as you see it?"

She answers so promptly that I can see she has already faced The Pill in our community, which is a good average one, some people rich, some poor, and most in between.

"The real reason," she says, "is that mothers and fathers just don't want to bother with their children. Oh, leave out the fathers—they never did want to bother! But now the mothers don't want to bother. They don't ask where their girls are going or with whom, nor do they set a time when the girls must be home. I know these mothers! They are so busy with their own lives, their jobs, their parties, their clubs, that they'd rather just provide The Pill for their daughters. And the daughters know it."

I remember the two ladies in the drawing room. Yes, they are busy with their own social life.

My daughter is talking, impetuous, earnest, angry. "And even worse," she goes on, "some mothers think that if their daughters don't have a boy after them, they lose status. Why, I know a woman here in our own community—I won't tell you her name—but she is long past the age of needing The Pill for herself. Yet only the other day she got The Pill from her doctor because her daughter, in two or three weeks, is going away on a camping trip with some other young people. The girl is not at all pretty and she doesn't often have a boy friend, and her mother wants her to 'have fun,' she said, so she gave her The Pill. What can young people do if their parents are like this—especially their mothers? Of course young people won't have standards if the older ones haven't any."

I am cruel enough to remind her, though gently, of certain incidents when she was a young girl and a beautiful one. "Remember the arguments you and I used to have? You were—and are—a wonder of an argufier!"

She laughs. "Of course I remember! And that's why I say what I do. I'm old enough now to know you were right. I knew it even then. I think I felt proud that you cared enough about me to insist on knowing the boy, the

place, the time I was coming home. Oh, you were . . .
and are . . . a wonder of an insister!"

So what is the new morality? Simply that while customs
may change, eternal principle holds.

The eternal way is to hold fast to the simple and
profound principles of integrity of the self and respect for
others. There can be no integrity for the self except as it is
based on discipline, self-discipline, the controlled and
regulated life, the proper balance between the physical,
the mental and the spiritual being. Overemphasis on any
one of the three aspects of the human being destroys the
balance of the whole and damages the personality
thereby. Respect for others? It means that one should do
nothing which destroys this same balance in another human personality.

Vague? I think not! Within each of us is the knowledge
of what the true self can be. The final law and commandment of the new morality remains what it has always
been. There is nothing new under heaven. Long ago
someone said, "To thine own self be true." And long ago a
little man named Immanuel Kant gathered into a compact
sentence the great Moral Imperative. Whatever you do,
he said, in effect, judge first whether you would be willing
for everyone to do that thing. The essential word is
responsibility—responsibility to oneself, responsibility for
one's every act and its result upon the self, one's own and
that of others. This is the eternal way.